"From the onset Sara informed me that she would mold her work first to satisfy herself. I suspect she's pleased. Next she felt she had something to say. And so she did. She wᵉ-plus-years of experience and accu   of career aspirants. And so she has. S   ᵒn for a demanding job must obvious   y right. Lastly, books are usually pro   ᵤᵢ ιove. She has that and so she composed. She effectively encourages aspirants attracted to the 'word trade'. She would take great delight to learn that she had inspired even a handful of you. Such an evoked joy would be no surprise to those of us who have known the ever-ebullient Sara."

R. Paul St. Amand, MD, author of
"What Your Doctor May Not Tell You About Fibromyalgia"
and *"What Your Doctor May Not Tell You About*
Fibromyalgia Fatigue"

"A superb little tome that entertains and informs. Sara tells it like it is, cleverly bringing to life the world of medical transcription, a little known but vitally important cog in the wheel of medicine. A delightful read for anyone fortunate enough to open its pages."

W. Grant Stevens, M.D., F.A.C.
Director, Marina Plastic Surgery Associates
Associate Clinical Professor, USC School of Medicine
Clinical Instructor, UCLA School of Medicine

You're a Medical What?!

A LIGHTHEARTED PEEK INTO THE WORLD OF A MEDICAL TRANSCRIPTIONIST

Sara Burns

Robert D. Reed Publishers
P.O. Box 1992
Bandon, OR 97411
Phone: 541-347-9882; Fax: -9883
E-mail: 4bobreed@msn.com
Website: www.rdrpublishers.com

Editor: Tim O'Rourke
Illustrators: Joe Kohl & Justin Thornburgh
Cover Designer: Mait Ainsaar, BICN Marketing & Design
Typesetter: Mait Ainsaar, BICN Marketing & Design

ISBN: 978-1-934759-00-4

Library of Congress Control Number: 2007938917

Manufactured and Printed in the United States of America

To my children, Greg and Amy Long, and to my husband,

Dee Burns, for distinctly disparate reasons.

ACKNOWLEDGMENTS

$\mathcal{T}$o embark upon even a relatively small project such as this, one must be motivated, driven and inspired, and must at all times remain excited about the process. It has taken me many years to arrive at this point, where I feel I have something to say that someone else might be interested in reading. To give credit appropriately would be to name everyone who has inspired and encouraged me for 29 years. This I cannot do. Instead I can only give a cumulative salute to all those good people who were there along the way. Thanks to all of you; you know who you are.

Having said that, there are a few who stand out, beginning with my junior college English literature teacher, the first person who told me that I should consider writing as a profession. (I was stunned!)

The next big thank you goes to the editors at JAAMT, who had faith in me and deemed my writing worthy of publication in their journals.

I am highly grateful to my editors, one of whom wishes to remain anonymous. *You know who you are and how much I*

appreciate your help in polishing this book. Working with you was such a joy. I am so proud to include two members of my family here. My step-grandson, Tim O'Rourke, who recently received his master's degree in journalism at the University of Oregon, and is launched on a most promising career, graciously agreed to co-edit the book. My grandson, Justin Thornburgh, a talented artist with an abundance of potential, happily came on board. (Thanks to both of you guys for agreeing to become involved in your grandma's creative endeavor.) Justin created the concept and style for the illustrations, and a professional illustrator fleshed them out. I hope this is only the beginning for Justin. A posthumous thanks to my former, late husband, Bill Hallam, who was with me through the often frustrating birth of my transcription career. His encouragement gave me the momentum and confidence I often needed in those early days.

In the midst of my gratitude, I also lovingly acknowledge my immediate family. First, my daughter, Amy Long, who has done me so proud by following in my footsteps and becoming, you guessed it, a medical transcriptionist — and not just any medical transcriptionist, but a very good medical transcriptionist. I clearly understand now the pride one feels when putting up that sign in front of the store that says "Jones and Son." Hard to explain — it just feels good.

Secondly, my son, Greg Long, without whom I would not even be a medical transcriptionist. He is my glue, my computer guru. He keeps my equipment running, answers all my dim-witted questions, advises and guides me in every aspect of the technical side of my work, somehow managing to do it with infinite patience.

Finally — last but not least — I wish to honor my husband, Dee Burns, my partner and soul mate. Dee listens to my incessant rambling about details of the business and calms me when things get frantic. He never questions my work priorities and never asks

"why." He simply leaves the room and lets me have at it. Night after night he sits at the dinner table, smiling and trying to enjoy his dinner, as I regale him with all the gory details of an emergency room drama I have just transcribed. Finally, Dee at all times and under all circumstances, says, "Honey, I am so proud of you." It does not get any better than that. Were it not for that support, these pages would be blank.

TABLE OF CONTENTS

FOREWORD

$\mathcal{S}$ometimes people write books from vanity, but truly have nothing to say. "Look at me: I'm an author." Sometimes they hype and tangle words, create nothing yet think they'll earn a few dollars. Sometimes they produce a tome surfeit with references and annotations that easily exceed anything meaningful in the text.

Sara has well avoided those pitfalls. From the onset she informed me that she would mold her work first to satisfy herself. I suspect she's pleased. Next she felt she had something to say. And so she did. She wanted to offer her score-plus-years of experience and accumulated wisdom in support of career aspirants. And so she has. She knew that her own passion for a demanding job must obviously exist in others. She is likely right. Lastly, books are usually produced as a labor of love. She has that and so she composed.

I've known Sara for thirty-four years and occasionally I've glimpsed how she thinks. My early observations concluded that she was one among a select few. She would actually look lovingly

at typewriters and later, at keyboards that were hooked up to all kinds of apparatus. Sara would nearly caress such machines and, through some seductive aptitude, get them to work her magic. The joy of striking keys to create words provided an allure that never left her. In this book she alludes to her ultimate skills, but she doesn't gloss over her apprentice ineptitudes.

She was gifted with the ability to type and think sequentially while using well-constructed, English grammar. Those dual assets were the basic talents she used to forge her career. Her struggle to etch medical lingo into her facile brain is nearly epic. Equipment got progressively more adept as did our Author and predictably, they wedded. Woman and machine, often ploddingly, somehow learned to decipher most of the challenging mumbles of her physician-clients.

The approaching death of her husband, my patient, prompted Sara to leave the balmy hospital environs of an air-conditioned record room. Bill needed terminal care and she unhesitatingly set up a quasi-sweat shop in a backroom of her home. In those days she did seem daunted and a bit frightened. The move and loss of job security made her question the sanity of making such life-altering changes. Yet she retreated from her nested safety and, remarkably, her fears were quickly tamed. Relief came swiftly as doctors almost eagerly grasped for her transcriptional skills.

Long before there was a "spell-check" Sara had made rag candidates out of more than one medical dictionary. She was driven to buy any book that would facilitate her transition from neophyte to enthroned transcriptionist. She asked for help from many sources and most people gave it freely. Her delightful personality was certainly no hindrance. She would phone someone and grapple with sounds and letter arrays that existed in no known language. The so assembled garbling eventually suggested something in English prose and germane to the dictation. Those were her victories.

Sara was never content just to learn a new word. She kept lists of those previously unknown to her. Included were names of diseases, medications, procedures, and esoteric terms common to physiology and biochemistry. She carefully recruited teachers from our medical ranks as she expanded her talents and ascended to another level. As I expected, she soon wanted to know what caused this or that condition; what bodily reactions accounted for some vague process; what might be the prognosis of such and such. Thus, continued her aspirations and then it happened. Sara had so well evolved into her long-coveted state of professionalism that she certainly deserves the title 'Master Medical Transcriptionist.'

Her progress did not always come in leaps and bounds. She well describes her apprehensions, struggles and tears for those of you with curiosity about her field. This book emotes some of those anguishes that she carefully threads through most chapters. However, her autobiographical foray is truly exuberant when she successfully expresses the deep love she has for her job. Thus, she effectively encourages aspirants attracted to the 'word trade'. She would take great delight to learn that she had inspired even a handful of you. Such an evoked joy would be no surprise to those of us who have known the ever-ebullient Sara.

R. Paul St. Amand, M.D.
Associate Clinical Professor
Medicine-Endocrinology
Harbor/UCLA

Author of
What Your Doctor May Not Tell You About Fibromyalgia
and *What Your Doctor May Not Tell You About Fibromyalgia Fatigue.*

PREFACE

*T*hroughout this book, for the sake of brevity, I refer to transcriptionists in the female gender, though some of the best transcriptionists I know are men. So, let it be known to one and all, my grammatical expediency is not meant to overlook nor neglect the contributions made by our male counterparts.

I use equal literary license when referring to physicians. For the most part, I refer to them in the male gender, though in 2004, 50% of entering medical students, and 45% of the graduating class, were women. So again, I use this grammatical tool only to simplify and in no way to discriminate against our most capable female physicians.

INTRODUCTION

*A*s this book goes to print, the world of medical transcription is in a tremendous state of flux. The changes whiz by like a racecar. Don't blink... you are sure to miss something significant.

In all the years I have been in this business, I have never seen so many rapid and profound changes in such an incredibly short period of time. It is a challenge to stay current and remain on the cutting edge. Seasoned transcriptionists, as well as newbies, should embrace these changes; they are not a threat to our job security but rather a major shift in emphasis.

Medical language specialists will be needed more than ever as these transformations settle in. While perusing this book, keep in mind that much of it was history before the ink dried, an almost nostalgic perspective of our world.

This is not a training manual, nor a definitive resource book for prospective transcriptionists, though I believe there is good information here for those seeking it. It is meant to be a lighthearted, eclectic compilation of thoughts and ideas that have surfaced as a result of my satisfying and rewarding career as a medical transcriptionist, plus a few experiences along the way that made this journey so intriguing. However, if someone, out of curiosity, randomly thumbs through these pages and feels a spark, has that urge to delve further into this strange amalgam of words and medicine, and is inspired to pursue this most interesting career, I will be delighted.

I have intentionally targeted three categories of readers: First, the veteran medical transcriptionist; second, those who are contemplating a career in medical transcription; and last, any inquisitive individual who happens upon this book.

I think transcriptionists never tire of exploring new avenues of learning, always searching for a fresh approach or a new morsel to help move their days along, or simply a little easy reading about one of their favorite subjects. So, this book is definitely for you.

To the readers who have an interest in transcription as a career, this book is also for you. Perhaps you have a vague knowledge of this profession and want to know more. I know from my own experience with random inquiries from friends, relatives and acquaintances over the years, there are many people looking for a new beginning, those who have seen and heard bits and pieces about our profession and who are hungry for more information. I wanted this compilation of diverse ideas, thoughts, experiences and advice to touch you, give you an inside look at the world of a medical language specialist. By the time you complete this little tome, I hope you will feel you have glimpsed enough of what it is we do and how we do it, to help you make an informed decision as to whether or not you really want to pursue a career as a medical transcriptionist.

Finally, for those of you who randomly picked up this book and were interested enough to open the first pages--having ventured this far, please venture on. I hope you find it an enjoyable ride.

TRANSCRIPTIONISTS DEFINED

$\mathcal{T}$ranscriptionists are the silent partners in the medical world. The service we provide is vitally important to everyone's good health. Without transcriptionists who are dedicated to absolute accuracy and strict confidentiality, the entire health system would descend into chaos. Without accurate, timely, and accessible records, continuity of care would be compromised.

The next time you visit your doctor or go to the hospital, keep in mind that somewhere behind the scenes, every aspect of your visit is being meticulously and accurately recorded by a dedicated and conscientious medical language specialist. Some day your life may depend on how well we do our job.

I would stand at the door between the recovery room and the surgical suite and lean in so far I would nearly fall over!

CHAPTER 1

A Little Background...
How Did I Get From There To Here?

"What do you wanna be when you grow up?" A universal question... with as many answers as there are individuals asking. How many of us actually end up fulfilling our prediction? Circumstances, events, and all of life's changes intervene and we often take a sharp right turn, finding ourselves miles away from our original dream or plan or wish. The answer for me, way back when, could not have been more predictable. Grow up, get married, raise a family. Suffice it to say, I was going nowhere in particular.

As usually happens, fate stepped in. In retrospect, I should have seen the signs. For some reason, I was always drawn to all things medical. Whereas most people dread entering a medical facility even to visit a friend, I was always excited, fascinated and, oh, so curious. At age 16, I landed a part-time job in a doctor's office and I knew I was in my element. The doctor was new in town and was applying for surgical privileges at a nearby hospital. Even back then, the documentation was intense and the doctor's wife was in the process of typing out long sheets of her husband's surgical history. I could not keep my nose out of it. I was drawn to it like a bear to honey. One day when I was alone, with nothing to do (this was before physicians' offices became insanely busy and chaotic), I hooked on those ancient heavy headphones and plunged into the documentation project on my own, looking up every word. There was no spell check — actually, no computer either — just a clattery old typewriter. It was such fun! I loved every minute of it — the challenge, the satisfaction of finally finding a word. I was spellbound. It satisfied some deep need in me. In spite of all this, it still did not hit me that this was the obvious course my life should take.

A few years later I became a volunteer at a large new hospital in our area. Again, my goodness, the joy I felt each time I walked in to do my job. In those days, "the job" included, (believe it or not), taking temperatures and pulses, and even giving back rubs! Nevertheless, I was still oblivious to the obvious.

Several years passed and the empty nest syndrome hit. I once again was drawn to what I loved ~ a hospital. I signed on as a volunteer and was immediately placed in the recovery room. My primary job was to precisely fold and wrap stacks of clean linens of various shapes and sizes, used in surgery to drape the patient and serve other purposes during the surgical procedures. I must have folded and wrapped thousands of lap sponges. These are not really sponges but rather 18-inch squares of multi-layered soft cotton, all sewn together, looking much like a tiny diaper (they made wonderful dust cloths and were in great demand once they were put out to pasture because of a tear or flaw). They are used primarily to pack a wound during surgery to soak up blood — not a pleasant thought, but still an essential element in the surgical process. It is hard to imagine now, but at that time there were no disposable supplies — everything had to be folded, wrapped, and

finally sterilized in an autoclave, to be used over and over. Here I was, in the middle of it all. I was ecstatic! Surgery was just steps away. The sanctum sanctorum! I was captivated. I would stand at the door between the recovery room and the surgical suite and lean in so far I would nearly fall over. There was nothing that did not amaze me. My curiosity was abuzz. The staff finally took pity on me, dressed me up in scrubs, and led me across that magical, mysterious, wonderful line into the "World of Surgery." I could barely breathe. I may have appeared calm and in control, but inside I was exploding with excitement. My enthusiasm knew no bounds. I did not want to leave at the end of the day.

Having finally crossed that all-important threshold, I eventually ended up at the surgery secretary's desk, absorbing it, taking it all in. I began filling in when the secretary went to lunch, then later expanded to filling in when she was ill or on vacation. I cannot describe the feeling I had, being a part of that team. It just felt right. I belonged to something very special, something mysterious to the outside world. I was part of a unique, exclusive team. When I went to the cafeteria for lunch, I nonchalantly took my place at the table that was unofficially reserved for "the surgical crew." I was in heaven. (For more on my experiences in surgery, please see Appendix B "The Sanctum Sanctorum.")

At one point I was asked to help in the medical records department, and lo and behold, there were transcriptionists! I had only vaguely heard of a "transcriptionist." (A significant comment here… note the word "transcriptionIST." We are very touchy about that word. We have been and are still regularly called "transcribERS," and we take umbrage to that. It may be picky, but to a transcriptionIST, it is important. A "transcribER" is a machine. We are "transcriptionISTS." Just wanted to clear that up right at the start.)

Again, curiosity took over and I quickly learned the role transcriptionists played in the whole scheme of things —

documenting and recording every aspect of a patient's experience from the moment of admission to the hospital until the moment of discharge. Although I returned to my beloved surgical suite, became a full-time surgical secretary, (and loved every single minute of it!), I could not get those transcriptionists out of my head. That windowless transcription room (and yes, they were actually upstairs, not in the basement) beckoned. I finally had my chance one day to try it out — it was remarkable. I was transported back to the days in that doctor's office, when I was 16 years old. Those words poured into my ears and flowed out my fingertips and, voila! A complete medical report appeared on the page. It felt good. It was clearly where I belonged. I had finally found my future.

Thus, my career began. I embarked on the long arduous task of amassing practical experience. (I would probably be appalled if I could look back and see some of my earliest work.) One of the biggest dangers of a transcriptionist who is just beginning the journey in the field of medical language is not so much the word that she cannot hear at all, but the word she thinks is correct, so never questions. The road that eventually leads to confidence and experience is, unfortunately, laden with all kinds of dangers and potholes. Thanks to my very patient fellow transcriptionists and a terminology class at a local college, as well as what I picked up in surgery, I slowly built up some basic knowledge of medical language.

When it became obvious that this was my calling, I signed up for additional classes that would give me the tools I needed to do my job well. A complete program gradually began to take shape, a series of courses that I felt were relevant to my career, including anatomy, physiology, pharmacology and business English. Since the college had only a rudimentary program relative to medical transcription (the terminology class) it was obvious to me that other subjects relating to the field of medicine would be of great benefit to a career in transcription. This

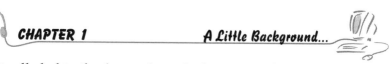

eventually led to the formation of what seemed to me a complete package, and I approached the college with the suggestion that it be formed into a new major curriculum, Medical Transcription. The idea was well received. I combined those courses with the standard college courses required for graduation, and eventually was the first student to graduate with an AA degree with Medical Transcription as my major. There was no turning back now.

While I was still getting my feet wet in the transcription department of the hospital, I encountered what I have always considered to be a truly serendipitous event. The group of physicians in the medical building across the street from our hospital had, for quite a long time, been using the transcriptionists in the hospital for their private office transcription, (free of charge, no less). When this was finally brought to a halt by hospital administration, guess who just happened to be right there, with everything already in place, to fill the vacuum created by this sudden turn of events. Talk about being in the right place at the right time. At that point, I made what was probably the most significant decision I have made in all my years in this business. I went way out on a limb and purchased a very expensive dictating machine that could be connected to outside phone lines (a relatively new concept at that time), and set it up in my new home office. It was a large, cumbersome machine that turned out to be a wonderful workhorse for many years. With all the new technology these days, that system seems archaic, but at that time it was "state of the art," and was a tremendous addition to my business setup. The doctors could use any standard phone, and by utilizing the push buttons, they were able to dictate, stop, back up, pause, listen to their dictation — all the same functions that a hand-held dictating unit could do. This dictation was recorded via the phone lines directly onto tapes in my machine. All I had to do was insert the recorded tapes into my handy little transcribing machine, and in no time the doctors had their completed reports.

Therefore, when all those desperate doctors suddenly had the rug pulled out from under them, (when the hospital stopped providing free transcription service for their private offices), I simply stepped in, presented my fresh new business card and, practically overnight, I was a home-based independent contractor.

I am clearly cognizant of the fact that this could not, would not, will not happen to everyone seeking a medical transcription career. I would even go so far as to say it probably never has and never will happen to anyone else. Yet, in retrospect, I give myself more credit than merely being in the right place at the right time. Had I not conducted my business in a proper manner, had I not been quick and resourceful, had I not produced an exemplary product for all those doctors, it would have been all for naught. But, because I was quick and resourceful, because I did conduct my business wisely and did provide outstanding quality, I did acquire those accounts and retained most of them for many years. In fact, my one plastic surgery account is still with me 29 years, two moves, and a year in Kauai later. It is obvious to me that the dual lesson here is to watch for every opportunity, and when something wonderful is handed to you, knock yourself out to take advantage of it and make it work for you.

The leap from being a transcriptionist to writing about being a transcriptionist seemed to sneak up on me. As I have indicated in my Acknowledgements, my English literature teacher planted the seed many, many years ago. She suggested I consider writing as a career. Writing... me? It had never, ever occurred to me that I was capable of putting together a coherent sentence, especially a sentence that anyone would have the slightest interest in reading, unless I was typing someone else's words. I tucked that surprising remark away and a few years later I was told the same thing by an English 101 teacher. After receiving complimentary remarks about a eulogy that I wrote for my grandmother's funeral, I realized this idea about writing was getting serious.

One day, I finally found the courage to put together an article and submit it to the editors at JAAMT (Journal for the American Association for Medical Transcription). To my utmost astonishment, it was accepted. I cannot tell you what joy I felt getting that first phone call, telling me the article I had submitted was actually going to be published in the next edition. Ultimately several of my articles have been published, and the thrill is new and fresh each time. Some of these articles are included in this book.

Is there another book lurking somewhere in my brain? I doubt it, but who would ever have imagined there was even one? In the meantime, I continue my journey as a medical transcriptionist.

It has been nearly 30 years, and I am still counting. Like all rides, there have certainly been some bumps along the way. I have never had any misgivings about the path I eventually took. (I must confess, however, those surgical suites still beckon to me from time to time.)

I have primarily been a stay-at-home independent contractor, have had numerous doctors' offices as clients, as well as some larger clinic and hospital accounts. I have trained a few willing souls who all went on to become successful independent contractors themselves. I have struggled with subcontractors from time to time, but mostly have just rolled along on my own. All in all, it has been a comfortable ride, and I have never, ever doubted that this was the journey I was meant to take.

I am nearing retirement. As the last chapter will tell you, I am not sure retirement will ever completely happen. This has surely been the right choice for me; I cannot imagine a life without the challenge of deciphering some doctor's dictation now and then. Picking up those familiar earphones and

connecting with that magical world of medicine still has a tremendously powerful tug for me. One thing for sure, I found the true answer, for me at least, to that important question, "What do you wanna be when you grow up?" I wanna be a medical transcriptionist.

CHAPTER 2

Everything You Always Wanted to Know About Medical Transcription
But Didn't Even Know What Questions to Ask

You are a what? I know this question is coming as sure as I know I can spell gastrojejunoesophagostomy. I am a medical transcriptionist. There are approximately 200,000 of us in the United States alone, and a rapidly growing number throughout the world. Yet, few people are aware of our existence, and fewer know the intimate and vital role we play in so many lives. We are medical language specialists, and we transcribe medical/legal documents.

Let us say you have chest pains and go to the emergency room. The doctor examines you and must then dictate a full report including your medical history, physical examination, the circumstances surrounding the event, and the treatment you receive in the emergency room. Now let us say you are then admitted to the hospital. The admitting physician must then

dictate an Admitting History and Physical Examination, covering essentially the same information that was in your Emergency Room Report. While you are in the hospital, the admitting physician calls in a cardiologist who examines you, and then dictates a Consultation Report. He decides you should have an angiogram. He then dictates an Operative Report, describing every detail of the procedure. You may have radiological studies, or the need for pathological analysis. In each case, a separate report must be dictated. Finally, you are discharged, and your physician must dictate a Discharge Summary, summarizing your entire hospital stay. The transcriptionist is on the receiving end of every one of those dictations.

Every time you walk into your doctor's office, you are generating a plethora of paperwork, much of which is transcribed by medical language specialists. This can include progress notes or chart notes, office surgery reports, letters to fellow physicians, letters to insurance companies on your behalf, or any other report (or correspondence) your physician deems necessary.

Some transcriptionists work in hospitals or clinics, some in transcription service centers, while others work at home. National transcription services abound and the current trend, though not altogether welcomed nor even endorsed by the transcription community, is to outsource transcription services to foreign countries, i.e., the Caribbean, India, and many other far-flung places.

A transcriptionist in India, working for a transcription service based in California, can now transcribe a report that was dictated by a physician in Ohio. From the time the doctor speaks the words until the final report is generated can be a matter of hours or less. (If you would like to learn more about this new technology, refer to Appendix A.)

Regardless whether transcriptionists work in a clinical

setting or a home setting (or even abroad), fundamental skills and training are required to do this job well. In order to understand and decipher what physicians (not always very clearly) dictate, transcriptionists must be knowledgeable in every aspect of medicine including medical terminology, anatomy, physiology, pharmacology and nutrition. Additionally, transcriptionists must be familiar with every medical specialty. They must also have excellent grammar, punctuation, editing and computer skills.

Quite frequently, overworked and overly tired physicians dictate something in error (i.e. starting the report talking about the *left* leg and it magically becomes the *right* leg). Transcriptionists are trained to identify these errors and to correct them. Thus, physicians never suspect that errors were made.

Transcriptionists wishing to work as independent contractors would do well to acquire experience in settings such as hospitals or clinics, where help is always available, before striking out on their own.

To become certified, transcriptionists must have at least three years' experience in a hospital setting. This simply qualifies one to take the examination. Of those who take the exam, approximately 60% pass and go on to become a CMT, or Certified Medical Transcriptionist.

I have been a medical transcriptionist for over 29 years. I work in my home and my current client list includes plastic surgeons, a county mental health clinic and two hospital emergency departments. Physicians dictate, through standard telephone lines, onto a digital dictation machine in my home office. This dictation is then accessed by me, using a piece of equipment usually referred to as a "C-phone," (AKA "voice processor") which looks much like a standard telephone. It is programmable and is connected directly to my dictation machine. This dictation system can also be accessed by other transcriptionists off site, again using standard telephone lines and C-phones. This allows me to utilize the services of subcontractors. Finally, using my C-phone, I am able to access offsite dictation systems in other cities, again through standard phone lines. I transcribe the appropriate reports, and deliver my completed reports either by email or by modem to the respective hospitals or clinics. This has allowed me so much flexibility that several years ago my husband and I packed up all my equipment and moved to Kauai for a year. I was able to continue with my private clients without a break, but with a decidedly different backdrop.

Transcriptionists are the silent partners in the medical world. The service we provide is vitally important to everyone's good health. Without transcriptionists who are dedicated to absolute accuracy and strict confidentiality, the entire health system would descend into chaos. Without accurate, timely, and accessible records, continuity of care would be compromised.

So, the next time you visit your doctor or go to the hospital, keep in mind that somewhere behind the scenes, every aspect of your visit is being meticulously and accurately recorded by a dedicated and conscientious medical language specialist. Some day your life may depend on how well we do our job.

Sitting in a bathing suit at my computer, watching whales and dolphins frolic off shore... does it get any better than that?

CHAPTER 3

You're Doing What?
The Pitfalls and Rewards of Living Your Dream

It seemed to come out of the blue. One minute we were perfectly content with our lives, the next we were into the "what ifs" and "if onlys." What if one of these days we were too old to do anything but sit in our rocking chairs and reflect..."if only we had done this"... "why didn't we do that." We could not let go of it — it kept coming back in our quietest moments to torment us. And out of that unrest grew the seed of an idea that blossomed into an unforgettable odyssey.

As a self-employed, home-based transcriptionist of many years, I assumed I was rooted to this spot forever. Au contraire! As the adage says, "Where there is a will, there is a way." It was becoming apparent that there was, indeed, a will. To complete the picture, however, there would have to be a way. It would simply (simply??) require determination, flexibility, creativity, a sense of humor, an abundance of hard work (both physical and

mental) and bountiful courage. And yes, quite frankly, a small stash of cash — perhaps less than one would think.

And what did my retired husband and I decide we just must do before the ravages of time precluded such nonsense? Why, of course, what else, "Let's move to Kauai, Hawaii, for a year!" And so "The Plan" was launched. First of all, we had to fund it. Not even considering that it could not be done, we began our campaign to save, squeeze, extract every penny we could. It certainly was not an easy task, but our determination far outweighed any common sense dictating that it could not be accomplished. Not knowing any better, we accomplished it. Once that began to take shape, the serious planning began. Ah, the number of times we decided in a moment of panic or discouragement that this fine idea was in reality sheer folly. An abundance of road blocks, we-really-cannot-do-this moments, are-we-crazy flashes — they became a regular part of our daily experience. When one of us bogged down in despair, the other dredged up enough of the adventurous spirit to pull us both along. We gradually confronted each obstacle and found solutions, and the grand plan took on a life of its own.

It was soon evident that there were two major obstacles: Housing, and, of course, operating my business 3000 miles away. The only way to afford housing in Kauai was to acquire income from our housing here. So began our strategy to find suitable renters for our home for a year, intending to use that money to rent something suitable (we hoped) in Kauai. First problem solved. Well, perhaps not solved, but at least we knew what we had to do. A very daunting prospect it was indeed.

In the meantime, the second challenge loomed. How do I move my work? Fortunately, we were well on our way simply because I did not use tapes. A quick side note for the readers who are not aware of the transcription process. At that time, before all the amazing modern day electronic wizardry, almost all transcriptionists worked with cassette tapes. Their clients would dictate their reports onto tapes, the transcriptionists would pick up the tapes, take them to their homes or to their own offices, play them back on their transcription equipment, using headphones and foot pedals. The completed transcribed work would then be hand delivered back to the clients. However, I did not use tapes. My work came in by a toll-free 800 phone line, which I had established from the outset of my business, a long-ago decision that turned out to be most auspicious. With an 800 line, which I funded, clients could pick up a telephone virtually anywhere in the world, dial my 800 number, and dictate. This dictation would go directly onto a piece of equipment I had in my office that recorded this dictation onto, yes, tapes again. I would transcribe this dictation, and then deliver it back to my clients, either by hand delivery, by mail, and in some cases, by email. My clients would not care where I was, since nothing changed for them. If they had not been told, they would not have even been aware that the destination of their dictations had changed from Northern California to Kauai. There would be a few minor adjustments such as a three-hour time difference, and a couple of local clients, accustomed to hand delivery, who would have to wait a little longer for mail delivery. I arranged coverage as best I could for a three-week span of time, and the rest of the doctors had to bite the bullet and take a three-week break from dictating. Few doctors will cooperate to that extent, but fortunately many of mine were longstanding customers, plus they did not dictate daily chart notes, mostly letters, so they were able to follow the plan without undue inconvenience. I assured them that three weeks would be the maximum they would be without service, a commitment that turned out to be nearly impossible to keep.

Finally, the time came. We put our rental ad in the local paper. We got a few bites that nearly convinced us we were truly out of our minds (as, by the way, almost everyone believed). The candidates were definitely not what we had in mind, not anyone

we would want living in our home for a year, and they were quickly eliminated. Then, one day, three angels arrived at our door, a delightful couple with a teenage daughter, who fell in love with our home, and we fell in love with them. And our first hurdle was behind us.

Our next step was to make plans to move a busy, full-time transcription business — my computer, printer, fax machine, dictating equipment, the phone lines… oh my, the myriad phone lines, reference books, bookkeeping records and stationery supplies. Here again, past decisions proved useful. My husband, being the pack rat that he is, saves all packing boxes. So at least we had appropriate shipping boxes for most large items.

As we began to look ahead to the seemingly endless tasks that confronted us, we decided we had to devise some kind of method to stay organized or we would simply spin out of control. Somehow, the typical notebooks and outlines did not seem to be what we needed. So we made a flow chart and pasted it the entire length of our office wall. This was mid-spring and we had set a target date of October 1. It was one long sheet of paper, divided into squares, and there was one square for every day between the day we began until October 1. Each important task was charted in the appropriate place on our flow chart and it became our daily touchstone. At first, those little squares were comfortingly and deceivingly empty, but as October approached, the squares began to fill frighteningly fast.

As our dream was becoming a likely reality, it became time to share our intentions with those who would be most affected — my clients. We felt that a letter or phone call announcing this ridiculous plan just would not do, only a face-to-face explanation would suffice. Some clients were local, but some were in far-flung locations. So, off we flew, and one by one, we sat down with each client and broke the news. As expected, there were diverse reactions, from "You are doing what?" to simply "OK, what do I

need to do?" Aren't doctors wonderful? We eventually lost two local clients, but one scurried back when I returned home the next year, and the other retired in the interim. Another obstacle conquered.

Back to the housing situation. Now that we had our local housing dilemma solved, we switched our focus to Kauai housing. Of course, the Internet was invaluable. Numerous emails and phone calls later, we began getting a picture of what was there, what was possible, what was available and what we could afford. We added a subscription to the Kauai newspaper for more input, and by the time we were ready to go, we were well informed and ready to plunge.

Without question, the most confusing and labor-intensive aspect of this project was preparing the house and everything in it. We were oblivious as to how much "stuff" we had in cupboards, on shelves, and in drawers and cabinets. We were inundated with decisions, big and small. It was worse than moving. Every item had to have a place to go. We divided everything that we could lift into five categories:

1) Take with us on the plane
2) Leave in the house
3) Put in storage
4) Take to the thrift stores
5) Ship

There were days when we could not walk through a room for all the stacks of "stuff." Isn't it odd how different your home looks when you are seeing it through someone else's eyes? So many little repairs needing to be done, so much cleaning and sprucing up to do.

As D-Day (Departure Day) approached, we frequently bordered on near hysteria, but we were always able to pull back, laugh at the absurd situation we had gotten ourselves into, and carry on. I can only surmise that our end goal was the carrot on

the stick that kept us from insanity, plus the fact that we had come this far and could not turn back.

D-Day arrived, and we were down to a minute-by-minute time schedule. I transcribed my last report, and we disconnected a room full of machines. Cords, cords, cords! Being the non-technicians that we are, we labeled every wire and cord we disconnected, "A to A," "B to B," etc. How smart we are, how clever... or so we thought. Everything was marked, packed and shipped... 21 boxes in all, no small task. Then, off to the docks to ship our car, and finally we were on our way.

Just for added interest, there was one last minute glitch. (Were we being tested?) I had decided to take care of necessary medical checkups at home before heading out into unfamiliar territory. This included, of course, my annual mammogram. As luck would have it, the physician felt he needed additional studies. Since even this did not satisfy him, and we were literally ready to walk out the door, arrangements were made for me to continue the investigation once I arrived in Kauai. We barely unpacked in Kauai before I made my appointment to see a physician on the island. She sent me immediately to a large hospital in Honolulu, on the island of Oahu, for definitive treatment. I had additional studies performed with some of that hospital's more sophisticated equipment, and was enormously relieved to learn that we were merely dealing with benign cysts, I could fly back to Kauai and pick up where we had left off.

The saga continues 3000 miles later, and a world away. We had arranged for minimal housing until we could find our "perfect place." Our frantic search began. Three weeks sounds like an abundance of time… it was not. There is nothing like a hands-on look. As with any other advertising, what you see in the newspaper and on the Internet is not always what you get.

We quickly discovered, once we arrived, that one person's idea of a "tropical paradise" could mean many things. We knew we wanted to live on the south shore. The north side of Kauai is absolutely gorgeous, but the reason for that is the tremendous rainfall. We decided we could visit the north shore, but preferred to live in a climate where we did not have to run our outfit for the day in the dryer before we could put it on. That narrowed it down considerably, but we still were overwhelmed by the variety available. We also were determined to live right on the ocean, where we could look out our windows and actually see the water. Don't think that didn't kick up the going price! We kept searching. It seemed everyone knew someone who knew someone who had a rental available. Had it not been so hot, and had we not been in such a hurry, our navigation skills would have been hilarious. Did you ever try pronouncing Hawaiian words? Even as a transcriptionist, trained to ferret out words, spellings and pronunciations, those street names were impossible. I routinely butchered it, and usually ended up spelling out each street we came to, trying to match names on the street signs with names on the maps. They all looked alike.

We eventually, through an amazingly circuitous route, found a lovely condo, on the ocean, at a price that would not bankrupt us in the first three months. Unfortunately, the owner was trekking around some far-off country, hunting komodo dragons, and would not be returning for three months. We wanted that condo and were willing to wait. Obviously, we needed immediate housing. It was a little easier to find a condo for three months than for a year, and we quickly latched onto a really beautiful place just a short distance from the ocean. Had it been right on the ocean, it would have been ideal... but, of course, way out of our price range. Nevertheless, three weeks later, we managed to move into this temporary condo until our truly perfect place became available. Now we did everything in reverse... we picked up our car at the docks, (plus 21 boxes), unpacked, and tried to find homes for all our plugs. Sadly, we had not taken into consideration one important element...Kauai

humidity. By the time we were ready to reconnect, using our clever system, most of the stickers had fallen off. So, we were left to guess which wires connected to which machines. Trial and error, plus several phone calls for help, and we finally found the correct receptacle for each wire and cord. And business began again, not quite "without a hitch," but surprisingly smooth. It was hot, we were exhausted, but we were too excited to give it much notice, and we were finally living our dream.

Our first condo had a huge loft where I set up shop. One of the first problems was our envelopes in the printer. They came out wrinkled and rippled, looked like the old-time Marcel hairdos. We thought something was wrong with our printer, called the company, and were told it was just the moisture. We would have to run each envelope in the microwave for one minute before we printed it. When I needed an envelope I would put it in a little basket, lower it on a rope, whistle for my husband. He would put it in the microwave, zap it, put it back in the basket, tug, and I would pull it up and print. There is always a way. Those are the little memories that will last a lifetime. I still smile when I picture that scenario. The only other accommodation that had to be made for my work (aside from training the mainland office personnel not to call me at 8:00 a.m. their time, 5:00 a.m. my time) was a little pile of talcum powder by my keyboard. The humidity was so intense, my fingers would stick to the keys. I had to constantly dip my fingers in the powder. Small price to pay for paradise.

We eventually moved into our "permanent" temporary home, (yes, unplugging and plugging, packing and unpacking again) and at last all the preparation and effort, all the anxiety and turmoil, was abundantly worth it. Sitting in a bathing suit at my computer, watching whales and dolphins frolic off shore... does it get any better than that?

As the year progressed, it was continually evident to us

that this had truly been the right thing to do. We had made a tough, insane decision, against everyone else's better judgment. But we did not regret it for a moment. Now when it comes time to sit in those rocking chairs, instead of sadly ruminating over what could have been, "if only," "what if"...we will smile and share the memories once again of our adventure in living, our six months of preparation craziness, and our beautiful year in Kauai. Was it money and effort well spent? Absolutely! Would we do it again? In a heartbeat.

Is there a moral to this saga? You bet. Live your dreams. Just because you are a home-based transcriptionist, you are not necessarily rooted to the soil like a tree, especially in this age of electronic magic. Your lives will dictate a different course, based on very divergent personal circumstances. At least start with the premise that all things are possible, do not let in "I cant's," do not settle for the status quo, believe in yourself, allow yourself to get excited about a Grand Plan, your very own special odyssey that will thwart those "if only's" when you are in your own rocking chair. Definitely think outside that proverbial box, and go for it!

CHAPTER 4

Tidbits From 29 Years as a Home-based Medical Transcriptionist
What I Hope I Have Learned

This chapter is primarily for the experienced transcriptionist, but worth a quick perusal by anyone who is curious about the day-to-day world of a medical transcriptionist.

Did it ever occur to you how much you have learned in all your years in this remarkable business we are in? I do not mean the technical skills or vocabulary. I am talking about more subtle things, the practical stuff, the nitty-gritty of our day-to-day work--the kinds of things that we tend to take for granted, but things that help get us through all the hours we put into our work. After 29 years in this business, I like to think I might have a few morsels, tidbits and pearls of wisdom to pass along, just as I am sure you have. Some of them are old hat; some might be new to you; and many of them will simply be the kinds of ideas that make you think, "Hey, that's right. I hadn't really thought of it that way before." Since about 99 percent of my career has been home-based, this obviously will be tilted toward that segment of the business, and will be of less interest to the hospital-based and clinic-based transcriptionists. For us, the homebound souls, here is some of what I have learned. I hope these morsels will be of interest to you, and perhaps some will bring a smile.

Make lists, lots of lists.

No matter how long you are in this business, you will continue to come upon words that you have always misspelled.

Belonging to AAMT is useful, beneficial, worth every penny, and definitely the right thing to do.

We will never stop saying stupid things from time to time. Years ago I trained/mentored a very bright lady. One day she called and asked, "When a doctor dictates, '3 o'clock' or '6 o'clock' position on the nipple, how do you know whether it is a.m. or p.m.?" The words were hardly out of her mouth before she realized what she had said... and it took a very long time for her to live it down. So when you think you have made a fool of yourself, laugh, and move on.

Maintain an air of professionalism at all times. Dress the part, act the part, speak the part. You are constantly being judged.

Develop and maintain good relationships with front office staff. They are your best source for new accounts. And they frequently are the ones who make the major decisions that can affect you. They also serve as an excellent conduit to the doctor... and a good buffer between you and the doctor.

Never work more than two hours at a time before taking a break. Even a two or three minute walk, stretch or series of exercises will refresh you.

You learn correct spellings in the darnedest places. Years ago, for some unknown reason, I was spelling Corgard with two "a's" until I happened to see it spelled on the side of a cardboard shipping box in a hallway. Billboards and magazine ads are also wonderful sources for catching an occasional "Oops."

How did we ever live without stickies?!

Never pass up an opportunity to promote your business. You can acquire new accounts in the most unlikely places. Keep your eyes and ears open for opportunities, in elevators, while shopping, and most of all, in your encounters with your own physicians.

Never keep snacks within arm's reach of your work station.

Train your friends and family right from the beginning that this is your work place. When you receive personal phone calls, immediately establish that you are at work. If you are willing to take the time to chat, indicate that you are merely on a break.

Always look in Vera Pyle's book first.

A comfortable, ergonomically-correct chair is the best investment you will ever make. Do not settle for less.

We can never take time off like "normal people." My niece, who is an excellent transcriptionist, was called for jury duty. When she stated it would be an extreme hardship for her to serve, explaining her job as a medical transcriptionist, the judge, an arrogant type, asked, "So what do you do when you get sick?" Her answer was? "I go to the bathroom and throw up, then go right back to work again." The judge dismissed her.

Maintain an up-to-date library of reference books. It is an excellent investment.

Try to maintain good working posture. Choose a trigger as a reminder to sit up straight (e.g., at the beginning of each page of work).

Every time you take on a new client in a new specialty, you will feel ignorant, slow as a turtle, incapable of handling it, and you will want to give up. Don't. Buy a new reference book for that specialty, get out all your other reference books, allow plenty of time, stay in touch with a network pal and, before you know it, you will be sailing through those dictations as if you had been doing them for years. You will wonder why it ever seemed so difficult.

Do not rely on the Internet. You can find anything you want if you look long enough, and it may not be accurate. Always rely on the tried and true reference books recommended by AAMT.

Always have business cards with you, and make sure they are as professional as you can possibly make them.

Network, network, network. Constantly strive to make professional connections. They will be invaluable in so many ways (e.g., backup and coverage for vacations and illnesses, second opinions on ambiguous decisions, morale booster when things seem bleak, and most of all, help with "What on earth is he saying?")

Make The Style Guide your best friend. Periodically pick some pages and study them. Continually refresh and update your fund of knowledge.

When dictation sounds like gibberish, leave a blank and finish the dictation. Chances are the doctor will say the word again and it will be clear as a bell. If you still cannot decipher it, and have the time, leave it until the next morning. Nine times out of ten it will pop out at you and you will wonder why it had been so difficult to hear the day before.

Build up "brownie points." Always go the extra mile with your clients; then when you need a favor, they will be more inclined to cooperate.

When you finally do get away from your work, try not to think about it. Give your brain a break.

Use macros and word expansion programs profusely. Be creative. Use your imagination. Remember, every keystroke you program into a macro, autosave, autocorrect, or word expansion program is one less keystroke you have to make... over and over and over.

Strive to become a CMT and maintain your status.

Maintain a neat and organized work station. It will save you time in the long run.

Always use your most professional voice when speaking on the phone. Excellent phone manners are paramount to an ongoing professional image.

If you have a family, establish rules for your work time and stick with them.

Take every opportunity to promote yourself as a medical language specialist.

When people inquire about our profession, take the time to inform them as well as you can. Do not sugarcoat it, but do not scare them off. Encourage them.

Periodically touch base with the office staff and, if possible, the physician. Ask what you can do to make your relationship better, more efficient.

Offer to mentor new recruits. The best way to learn is to teach.

Never record silly or frivolous answering machine messages. Remember, this is your business and you are a professional.

When a physician's office shows interest in your services, impress them with a well-organized presentation, punctuality, and a professional demeanor. Look like a professional. Be ready to present to them all the materials they might request and more. Have answers to every anticipated question. If you do not know the answer, tell them you will get the answer, then do so, promptly.

Try not to work too often in your PJs (although it is so

tempting). Dress the part and your work will reflect it.

Proof, proof, proof! Remember, unless you are associated with a large transcription service, you are your own QA (quality assurance).

Establish your own personal "best time of the day." We all have one — are you a morning person, a night person? Then work like crazy during that block of time. Let nothing distract you, except your mandatory few minutes for breaks.

Always return business phone calls promptly. Put out fires, solve problems as quickly as possible.

Do not share your unpleasant tales and gory surgical details at the dinner table. It may be interesting to you, but spare the rest of the family.

Always imagine your client is reading your work in front of you. You will probably be inclined to produce better work.

When speaking with office personnel, be friendly, but brief and to the point. They are as busy as you and have neither the time nor interest in your personal problems.

Try to have backup equipment available in case of breakdowns. Failed equipment creates downtime most of us cannot afford.

Attend seminars, workshops, annual meetings and local chapter meetings as often as possible. They are invaluable tools for learning, refreshing your store of knowledge, networking and boosting your enthusiasm.

Maintain close ties with a "technical guru." They are your best friends when equipment goes haywire. (If your spouse is your guru, you are one very lucky person.)

Zip your lips and shred the evidence. In other words, take your confidentiality agreement very seriously.

Take advantage of AAMT's help line. They are knowledgeable, friendly and quickly responsive... and they want

to help.

If, through your work, you accidentally learn personal details about a friend or acquaintance, be surprised when you hear it from them. Never reveal that you have personal access to their records. (I often tell a little white lie when they ask if I have "typed" their report, and say that all my work is handled through patient numbers rather than names, so I have no idea who the patient is.)

Maintain your sense of humor. Some days that will be all you have to keep you sane.

When you reach your burnout stage (and we all do), dream a dream, create a wonderful odyssey and then make it happen. It can be something as small as a trip to the ice cream store, or as big as a plan to move to a new and exciting location, like Kauai, for instance.

I rest my case, but I am sure everyone who has spent much time in this business could add more. If you are new to our world of medical language, perhaps this has given you some insight into some of the details of a day in the life of a medical transcriptionist.

CHAPTER 5

The Symphony
An Imaginative Sojourn to Help You Through the Day

*E*ver wished you had an orchestra at your command? Ever thought about all those instruments that make up that orchestra? Well, sit back and I will create a full symphony for you. It's easy. They are all right there in your earphones. What? You haven't heard them? Just use a little imagination and listen along with me.

We will start with the tuba, Dr. Oompapa. Harrumph! I know you have come across him. Rumbling, mumbling deep voice, plenty of throat clearing, grunting and fussing about. "The incision was made with a...... crrummmph..... #11 blade..... puff, puff, no, #15 blade..." Can't you see that big tuba? And can't you picture Dr. Oompapa?

We move to the very front of the orchestra. The flute, Dr. Dulcidove. We have all had that twiddly sweet little voice in our ears, haven't we, where you have to turn up the volume a bit?

Dulcet melodious tones, well modulated. Never caught that lady in a cough. Little trills, lovely, strings of words up and down the scale. She always brings a smile to my face.

Rat-a-tat, rat-a-tat! There are your drums. Dr. Matsudrumdrum. He spits out his words, clipped, curt and precise, but quickly. Thrown out in quick bursts, terse and brusque, with endless pauses between, while we sit with our fingers poised. Pronunciation is his focus. Snap, slap, ping, ping. And our rhythm section is on a roll.

Can't let this symphony perform without your oboe. Irritating, sharp, Dr. Harshnarsh. Tones that clamor and grate in your ears, harsh, yammering, a strident, shrill song that we dread. We're usually happy when this little oboe interlude is over.

And what fun we have with our trombone, Dr. Honeytone. Up and down the scales, rich tones sliding, rolling, words undulating and swaying. We bend and lean with each phrase, find the rhythm and lose ourselves in the moment. This one can put us to sleep.

Want a perfect end to a musical day at the computer? Bring on Dr. Sexysax. Oooo. Mmmmm. We are transported to a steamy, smoky room, a soft piano in the background, sounds full and resonant. The words curve and slide, roll out in carefully formed, sensuous phrases, dancing slowly and rhythmically. Oops, his verb didn't match that noun. And we're jerked back to reality.

What a concert we had, huh? We do not need tickets to our command performance. It is all waiting for us in our trusty little headphones. So next time you sit down for a day of routine work, use your imagination. Getting bored? Bring out your orchestra. Welcome back Dr. Oompapa or Dr. Sexysax. What is that? A new addition? Great! Add him or her to your symphony. Bring in a new instrument. You will find that your boredom disappears and your day will fly by.

They never look anything like you had pictured them.

CHAPTER 6

No! You Can't Be Dr. Smith!
A Well-known Truth: They Never Look Like They Sound

*H*ave you ever transcribed hospital reports from doctors you have never met? Then you finally meet them? In this age of electronic communications, the chances of that are extremely likely. Even in my day, I had several instances where I had clients for over 20 years and never laid eyes on them. Biiiig surprise, isn't it? They never look anything like you had pictured them.

I transcribed reports for our local emergency room for several years and my least favorite dictator was a doctor who belched, chomped apples, and worse. Needless to say, I certainly had a preconceived notion of how he looked. I pictured an overweight, unkempt fellow, hair askew, scruffy beard, scrubs all jumbled and wrinkled, someone you would never want to encounter in a social situation. One evening my husband and I attended a social event at the local country club. We were seated at a table with this most adorable man. You guessed it, it was my

belcher. I nearly melted. He was not only the cutest doctor I had ever met, but he was genuinely the sweetest, kindest, most down-to-earth guy you could imagine. If I had not been happily married, I would have made a complete fool of myself over this gem. I quickly became so relaxed and comfortable with him, I even got up the courage to tell him he really should quit belching in our ears — he was that easy to talk to. He had never realized he did that, apologized and promised not to do it ever again. We ran into each other many times after that and he continued to be my very favorite doctor… in person. A real charmer.

Epilogue: He never stopped belching. I have to admit, after getting to know him, all those unpleasant habits somehow did not matter nearly as much!

I have always found it very difficult to hide my surprise when I finally am introduced to a doctor who has been "in my ears" for a long time, and one whom I had formed a solid preconceived notion of how he looked. What are you going to say if you pictured them ugly? "Oh, you are so much better looking than I thought you were." I don't think so! Obviously you are never going to say "Wow, you sure are not as nice looking as I thought you were." So, if you have a preconceived notion of how your clients look, get ready to present a completely blank face when you are confronted with an introduction.

Have you ever noticed how familiar and intimate you become with those voices? You learn to recognize every tiny nuance. In fact, I have a difficult time convincing my husband, but I can identify some of my clients simply by the way they take a breath. Really! I know you veterans out there will understand and agree with that, and you novices will soon believe it too. Some of my clients' voices become so familiar to me, I am able to tell when they are tired, when they are catching a cold, when they are annoyed or depressed, and a whole gamut of other day-to-day changes and emotions.

I had been transcribing for a small hospital for quite awhile and, as we all understand, I had my favorites and least favorites. There was one doctor's dictation (on tapes on those days) that we in the transcription department all schemed and worked to grab. I had never met this man. One day I was rounding a corner in the hospital corridor, heading to work, and I passed by a couple of gentlemen conversing. One of those voices nearly knocked me over. There was "The Voice," that voice that we all fought over. I bravely backed up, politely interrupted the conversation and asked, "Do you happen to be Dr. _____?" Of course it was. I had nailed it without a doubt. And in this instance, the face and entire appearance matched the voice perfectly. In fact, I often wondered if I could have picked him out had I not heard his voice. It was that obvious. And this lovely gentleman went on to be my mentor, my doctor, my counselor, and my very best friend. I guess you just never know what is around the corner.

CHAPTER 7

Ode to a Home-based Transcriptionist

*W*e work, we slave, it never ends,
Come up for air, then get the bends.

We work in our jammies, hair a mess,
No beauty queen, we must confess.

But quality work is still our goal,
Without a blemish, without a mole.

What IS that word, what DID he say,
We're way behind, must get through the day.

Oh, no, Dr. Mumbles, I simply can't take it,
Should I put it back, or can I fake it?

They keep droning on, it begins to blur,
Didn't I just hear him call "him" a "her?"

My fingers are tired, my back is sore,
This endless report is such a bore.

I think I'll stop and get a num-num,
A little snack to fill my tum-tum.

They are giving him CODEINE? Oh, no, that's not right,
He's allergic to codeine, he'll pass out like a light.

What is that noise? Is he eating his lunch?
MUST he dictate and continue to munch?

Screaming babies, TVs and cars,
Next thing you know, they'll dictate in bars.

Dr. Endless is next, dear me, time for lunch,
He will probably be dictating a whole great big bunch.

Why don't they SPELL that patient's name?
Don't they know that all names sound the same?

We continue to search until we drop,
For numbers and spellings that go on the top.

Time for a break, drank too much tea,
Can't wait much longer, I gotta pee.

Guess I'll go back, maybe hear it this time,
The way they mumble is such a crime.

Here we go, is it "lay" or "lie"?
I hope I learn that before I die.

At last, here is one I can actually HEAR,
He has a nice rhythm, so precise and CLEAR.

Don't stop! Keep them coming, I think I'm in love,
He must have been sent from heaven above.

Egads! It's QA time, I'm going to get fired,
Really and truly, I was just overtired.

What the heck is he saying, I'm up a tree,
Gotta call someone, now who will it be?

All we remote IC gals get along fine,
I'll scratch your back and you scratch mine.

We're lucky we hooked up with this wonderful crew,
We hope that the feeling is mutually true.

We're out in the boonies, they're big city folk,
We're sure glad they're there, and that's no joke.

It's really a problem when we get stuck,
Need someone to help us out of the muck.

We call them up, we can be a pest,
But they try hard to help, they give it their best.

There's no doubt about it, we love our job,
We're a very rare breed, a few in the mob.

If your computer monitor has at least 30 yellow sticky notes adorning the edges, you might be a medical transcriptionist.

CHAPTER 8

You Might Be a Transcriptionist Of...

*J*eff Foxworthy, a very popular comedian currently on television, has a well-known routine that goes something like this: "If _____ you might be a redneck." It occurred to me that I could come up with a similar routine, adjusting it to fit a medical transcriptionist. With an apology and a tip of my hat to Mr. Foxworthy, the following is my version of that familiar routine.

If every time you sit in any chair you automatically feel for the foot pedal with your foot, you might be a medical transcriptionist.

If you can spend two hours discussing the pros and cons of where to put a comma in a sentence...and that doesn't seem unusual to you...you might be a medical transcriptionist.

If you send your husband to the LUMBAR store for some hardware, you might be a medical transcriptionist.

If you can't read anything in print without instituting major editing, you might be a medical transcriptionist.

If you wake up in the middle of the night and suddenly know what that missing word was...and you just have to wake your husband to share the good news, you might be a medical transcriptionist.

If a gory emergency room story seems like perfect dinner table conversation, you might be a medical transcriptionist.

If every relative three degrees removed, and every friend and distant acquaintance, calls you for medical advice, you might be a medical transcriptionist.

If you jump out of your chair and do the hokey pokey because you just discovered a new medical term, you might be a medical transcriptionist.

If every time a friend tells you he or she is taking new medicine, and you just HAVE to know the name of it, you might be a medical transcriptionist.

If you have a second cousin who has a neighbor who is SURE she can be a "transcriber" because she worked in a pharmacy, and wants your advice on how to get clients, you might be a medical transcriptionist.

If you are developing a dowager's hump...and you are only 25 years old, you might be a medical transcriptionist.

If you walk through a hospital and suddenly exclaim "I KNOW that voice, I KNOW that voice," you might be a medical transcriptionist.

If you are the only one in the room who actually understands what that person with the thick foreign accent is saying, you might be a medical transcriptionist.

If your calves are the most developed muscles in your body, you might be a medical transcriptionist.

If your kids are writing a paper for school and they put it

on tape and ask you to have it ready to be turned in by tomorrow, you might be a medical transcriptionist.

If you can type and take a nap at the same time, you might be a medical transcriptionist

If you have the flu and a raging temperature, and it never occurs to you to stop working, you might be a medical transcriptionist.

If you have an almost uncontrollable urge to correct grammar during any conversation, you might be a medical transcriptionist.

If you choose your family doctor based on how well he dictates a sentence, you might be a medical transcriptionist.

If your husband tells you your fingers were "typing" in your sleep, you might be a medical transcriptionist.

If you make out your grocery list while you are transcribing a report, you might be a medical transcriptionist.

If the word "vacation" is not in your vocabulary, you might be a medical transcriptionist.

If you constantly talk back to the TV, correcting peoples' pronunciation of medical terms, you might be a medical transcriptionist.

If working in a windowless basement seems like a normal thing to do, you might be a medical transcriptionist.

If being called a medical transcribER makes the hair on the back of your neck stand straight up, you might be a medical transcriptionist.

If you spend more than an hour searching the Internet for just one elusive term, you might be a medical transcriptionist.

If a fellow transcriptionist calls and needs help with a word... and you actually know what it is... and your feet don't hit the ground the rest of the day, you might be a medical transcriptionist.

If your computer monitor has at least 30 yellow sticky notes adorning the edges, you might be a medical transcriptionist.

If a piece of equipment crashes, and you have an immediate anxiety attack, you might be a medical transcriptionist.

If a doctor offers you a compliment, and you wear an Alfred E. Newman grin for the remainder of the day, you might be a medical transcriptionist.

If you carry on a dialog with the doctor dictating in your ears, you might be a medical transcriptionist.

And finally, if you cannot imagine a life that does not include medical terms, hospitals, doctors and clinics, you might be a medical transcriptionist.

CHAPTER 9

In Defense of Doctors
Some Pros and Cons on the Balance Sheet

*W*e love them, we hate them. They are the blessings in our lives and the bane of our existence. They annoy us and irritate us, they amuse us, frustrate and bore us, they get on our nerves, they exasperate, infuriate and entertain us. They make us laugh, they make us cringe; they make us squirm and wince; they ruin our day, they make our day. We cannot live with them, and we cannot live without them. They are those amazing guys and gals who whisper, mutter, bellow, mumble, and yes, sometimes even just talk into our ears hour after hour, day after day. They chew gum, belch, chomp apples, snore, butcher the English language, and change left legs to right legs. They carry on conversations with others in the room, watch a ballgame on TV, bounce their screaming baby, all the while trying to dictate. They dictate in homes, cars, airports, airplanes, cabs, hotel rooms, poolside, and

occasionally even in their offices. They are the doctors who give us reason to do what we do. Unfortunately, they did not have the advantage of a "Dictating 101" class in medical school (certainly not a bad idea).

In the last 29 years I have interacted and interfaced on a daily basis with the "engines" of the medical world — the physicians. The first thing I learned was, there is certainly variety. There are the curmudgeons and the sweethearts; the perfectionists; the "regular guys" and the prima donnas; the tyrants and pussycats; those who will do anything to make your work easier and those who want you to do everything to make their work easier. I have had my battles with a few, days when I announced without question that I was going to "drop that account just as soon as I can find one to replace it,"… which I probably ended up actually doing only once or twice in all these years.

I was perusing a book of essays the other day and came across the following quote by Lewis Thomas. He was referring to scientists in particular, but I felt it applied to physicians as well, "I don't know of any other human occupation in which the people engaged in it are so caught up, so totally preoccupied, so driven beyond their strength and resources." It set me off on a journey of reflection. These guys (and gals) are really something special. Just think about it. If a carpenter puts a board in the wrong place, he merely says "Oops" or probably something a little more colorful, then fixes it. When an accountant makes an error in a client's books, it may cause some inconvenience, but usually it can be amended and everyone moves on. But let a surgeon makes a mistake, and he could very possibly kill or maim the patient. When a physician tells a patient to take medicine that is contraindicated, think of the consequences. Oh sure, doctors are not supposed to make those kinds of mistakes. Let's face it, though, our docs are human. They make mistakes and the consequences are often devastating. Physicians are stretched to their limits and beyond all the time. Our own annoyance level often reaches the top of the chart, but just think of the responsibilities that are on the doctor's shoulders. He or she is frequently exhausted, pulled in many different directions at once, wishing he or she were at home with the family or at least with a good book. I asked one of my clients years ago what he wanted most to do in life. His answer? Sit on the porch of his prairie home, feet on the banister, and smoke his cigar.

If it seems that I view the medical profession through rose-colored glasses, think again. My poor husband has had to suffer through years of my roller coaster moods with my clients. I recently ran across a little gem in a thrift store book stack, "MD, Doctors Talk about Themselves" by John Pekkanen. By the time I finished that book, I began to wonder why anyone would ever want to become a doctor, or why one would stay in the profession. Indeed, they are leaving in droves, for a variety of reasons. Most of them, thanks to Medicare/Medicaid changes and skyrocketing malpractice insurance rates, simply cannot afford to practice medicine anymore. Can you imagine devoting 8, 10, 12 years to professional education, only to find that when you go out into the real world, you can't even afford to stay in that field? Studies have shown that the majority of people who choose the medical profession actually do so because they have that Marcus Welby syndrome. They really are idealistic and just want to help people. Sadly, the real world turns out to be far from that image and doctors are giving it up.

So, let's walk in their shoes (okay, expensive shoes). Put yourself in their place and remember the burdens they drag around with them on a daily basis. Anytime you feel the urge to throw your earphones at the wall, remember — the doctor on the other end of the line may not have had a very great day either. He probably was making rounds before you even got out of bed, has a desk piled with paperwork and longs to be home. He might have made more life and death decisions today than you will make in a lifetime. He has possibly changed a few lives forever, has had to weigh pros and cons and make decisions that King Solomon himself would have shunned. So let's cut him some slack.

There is a strong caveat here. Regardless how weary or distracted our physician-clients may be, rudeness and lack of consideration are inexcusable. These people still have to interact with the real world, and there are lines that cannot and should not be crossed, even by them. If that line is crossed and a client is consistently inconsiderate or egregious, my advice to you is to drop that physician like a hot potato. Hopefully, when you find someone to take his place, it will be one of those wonderful dictators who appreciates you and all your efforts, one who, in spite of his tough day and a wealth of difficult decisions, will try his best to make your job a little easier.

However, if that line is not crossed, and you can work with the situation, grit your teeth and offer an occasional scrap of sympathy. Throw a little karma his way. You know what they say about karma. One of these days, right out of the blue, when you least expect it, you will hear in your earphones, "Thanks, transcriptionist, you're doing a great job and I really appreciate it." Ohmygosh! Your feet won't hit the ground for days, right?

So the next time you have to labor through a less-than-perfect dictation, with lousy grammar, imperfect syntax, yawns and mumbles, take a deep breath, put on some soothing music, mentally slip into the dictator's shoes, put a smile on your face and get the job done. Remember, that physician or one of his colleagues may save your life some day.

Transcriptionists are often subjected to some weird and wild stuff coming through their headsets!

CHAPTER 10

These are a Few of My (Least) Favorite Things
Why Do I Stay In This Business?

It doesn't take long, once you get into the meat of this business, to realize that there are some Universal Truths among all transcriptionists. Few are more common than our pet peeves and, conversely, the things that make us smile. The following are a few thoughts along those lines.

Physicians are a busy bunch, no doubt. They make life and death decisions every day and they carry around a tremendous burden of responsibility for the well being of their patients. They are, by necessity, completely absorbed in their work, in their day-to-day challenges, dilemmas and decisions. As a result, physicians, most of whom dread the chore of dictation, can easily forget that a live transcriptionist is listening at the other end of that line. Consequently, transcriptionists are often subjected to some weird and wild stuff coming through their headsets!

Eating while dictating seems to be a favorite. This occurs because they are so pressed for time, they have no time to eat otherwise. I am sure they never give a thought to the sound effects this creates. Apples are particularly noisy and juicy when magnified through earphones, and doctors love apples. You can almost count on missed words and phrases. "The patient was currunch, mmmphlaed shorrrshofss phaessspp — swallow.... in intensive care."

Chewing gum... need I say more?

Akin to chewing is the yawn. Yawns, in and of themselves, are perfectly acceptable. However, doctors must be well trained in medical school to never let an unproductive minute go by, so they invariably yawn and continue to dictate at the same time. The way I generally handle the situation is to type exactly what I have heard: "The patient's blood work came back with (yawn) abnormality." Alternatively, in some instances I call to clarify what was intended.

How about biological sound effects? While all humans are capable of strange bodily sounds, such sounds can be particularly amusing coming through the dictation line. Once again it seems that dictators frequently forget there are live, listening ears at the other end. This becomes especially entertaining when the transcriptionist must repeatedly rewind, listening again and again in order to decipher the obliterated word.

Did you know there are several categories of belches? Any transcriptionist will attest to this. There is the hiccup belch, the oops-I-didn't-mean-to-do-that belch, the bubble belch, and my all-time favorite, the rolling belch. I have actually encountered such creative belches that I thought it was a word, until I listened over and over and finally discovered that it was not, or alternatively, sometimes it was a word camouflaged nicely within the belch. The first few times a transcriptionist encounters a belcher, it is usually worthy of a "listen to this" if it is in a clinic or hospital setting. But it's amazing how, after awhile, the seasoned transcriptionist merely presses ahead with hardly a wince. It seems to prove the theory that you can adjust to almost anything.

Paper shuffling is a classic sound effect. It inspires images of desks piled high with reports, lab slips and miscellaneous papers. While dictating, our clients seem to be incessantly looking for something in those papers. It often seems that the dictation is just a few words ahead of the data they need, so they shuffle, sort, riffle, stack and generally manipulate all those volumes of paper. Of course, the sounds shoot straight into our ears.

In addition to the aforementioned examples, there are other factors that decrease sound quality. Muffled dictation results when a doctor hooks the phone on his shoulder in order to free up his hands while continuing to dictate. Doctors need more hands.

Some physicians pace when they dictate. That is fine, but wouldn't it be great if they carried their dictating device with them? They often lay it down and actually walk around the room and continue to dictate. Their voices fade in and out as they move toward and away from the dictating device. Occasionally, you will find a doctor who has such a resonant, clear voice, it really does not matter how much he moves around. You can hear and understand every word. I had one like that and it was such a joy. But oh they are rare!

Then there are the whisperers and boomers. You will always have a wide range of volumes if you are transcribing for several doctors, switching back and forth. You get the boomer who nearly blasts you out of your seat. Then, of course, your next one is the whisperer. Up goes the volume, you have to keep going back and listening again and again. Ever notice how you lean

forward when you cannot hear something? What is that all about? Why do we think we will hear it better if we lean forward? Anyway, we gratefully finish that report and tap into the next one. Yep… every time… another boomer, and your eardrums are not the same the rest of the day.

What about the physician who performs dual roles — he dictates, and he carries on a conversation with others within earshot, or occasionally not within earshot. I have actually transcribed a string of sentences, only to finally realize that I was transcribing extraneous social conversation rather than the medical report. Don't you hate it when the dictator laughs at something obviously humorous and he does not share it with you?

Once in a while, you will come across background noise that you want to hear. I had a client who loved classical and easy jazz music and always had one or the other on while he dictated. It was just loud enough that I could hear it, but not too loud to interfere with my ability to understand him. I cannot tell you how soothing it was to hear that music. In fact, it was so pleasant, I set up my own music, playing softly in the background. An excellent way to decrease stress. I highly recommend it.

Universal annoyances do not always fall in the category of the infinite variety of sounds that come wafting into our ears day after day. Transcriptionists take great pride in their work. Anything that hampers their ability to produce a quality document diminishes their sense of accomplishment. There are many roadblocks that a transcriptionist faces. For example, a dictation is not a race, but there are always those clients who strive to complete their entire dictation in one big breath. This almost certainly guarantees that the report will be full of errors and blanks, an outcome that is painful to transcriptionists and unacceptable to physicians.

Enunciation and appropriate pauses are essential tools

needed to achieve an excellent result. There is a direct correlation between the quality of input and the resultant output. Without clear and precise dictation, transcriptionists must spend an inordinate amount of time listening for tiny nuances and minute inflections to decipher what the dictator intended.

Transcriptionists sigh with relief when dictators remember to spell patients' names, both first and last. It is surprising how many names have multiple spellings. For example, to name a few:

- Allen/Allan/Alan
- Catherine/Kathryn/Cathryn/Kathrine/Katherine
- Stephen/Steven
- Jeffrey/Geoffrey
- Shawn/Sean
- Michelle/Michele

It doesn't stop with first names, either, although dictators do tend to spell more last names than first. How about Smith/Smyth, Jordan/Jordon, Larson/Larsen. On and on it goes.

Let us all give a big high-five to this one. The old one-two trick. In a diagnosis or other subject that may or may not include more than one item, dictators almost never say "One," so you assume there is only one, you set it up as a single item, and what invariably happens? It turns out to be a series and they go on to "Two." Sooo, you have to back up, set it up as a series, put in your "one," then "two," etc. The next time, when you put in "one," then set up for "two," assuming it will be a series, sure enough, it is a single and there is no "two." I have a feeling if I were dictating I would do the same thing. It all has to do with which side of that microphone you are on, and the last thing a busy physician needs to do is constantly think ahead and anticipate the pitfalls for the

transcriptionist on the other end. We do have macros, word expansions, all kinds of little tricks that can help out here, so it is but a minor annoyance. I mention it more because I am so puzzled that it is as prevalent as it is.

Are all you transcriptionists just waiting for this one? Spelling! If you are not yet among the ranks, you will soon learn this truth...you must never rely on a dictator's spelling. Medical school is charged with the task of stuffing an unbelievable amount of facts into the heads of their students, and spelling lessons are probably not paramount. The end result turns out to be a population of physicians in whom you trust your very life, but you cannot trust their spelling. Do not get the wrong impression. Many physicians are the epitome of fine grammarians, punctuators and spellers. A transcriptionist needs to always appreciate the fact that a good percentage of doctors are thoughtful enough to take the time to try to spell words they feel we need a little help on. However, your best plan of action is to always verify the spelling if you are not already sure that it is correct. Don't shoot the poor guy for trying... simply be grateful for his thoughtfulness.

And finally, the classic. As I mentioned in a previous chapter, physicians come in all kinds of packages. My experience has been that a huge majority of them are kind and thoughtful folks. But I need to mention a small category that, as I had said, want you to do everything necessary to make their jobs easier. One of the common practices among this very small group is the following: Dr. Jones dictates a report, then asks, or worse, insists, that it be transcribed immediately and returned immediately, as the attorney's office is waiting for it at that very moment. That is bad enough. No one enjoys transcribing a report under such time constraints. What is really difficult is when we find out, and we almost always do find out, that that letter was supposed to have been dictated two months ago and it has been sitting on the doctor's desk. I do not mind going the extra mile occasionally

when the doctor is in a pinch, but any experienced transcriptionist will agree with me that the "I need it yesterday... because I was supposed to have dictated it two months ago" syndrome is a major aggravation. Again, I reiterate, this represents a very small minority of bad apples, far outweighed by the sweethearts who would never think of pulling such a trick.

Just in case this chapter is beginning to sound like nothing but complaints, I want to end it with a few upbeat experiences I have had, just to prove that what we encounter on a daily basis is not all bad, not by any means. All in all, we learn to cope with the bad stuff and try to remember all those special moments that are uplifting and that make this profession the joy it is. Read on.

It truly makes my day when a doctor throws in a quick side comment to me, even just a "Thank you," or "Have a nice day." And when they include my NAME with that, as in "Thank you, Sara," I cannot get the idiotic grin off my face. I once had a doctor say, "I apologize for my cold... and Happy Thanksgiving." Such a simple thing, but warmed me to my toes. In fact, I immediately sent off an email to the head of the transcription department, told her exactly what he had said, and how it affected me. I got an email back, thanking me for mentioning it. She said she would forward it to the doctor as a "Touch-O-Gram." What goes around, comes around, and we all end up with warm and fuzzy feelings.

Have you ever had a doctor fall asleep while dictating? It happened to me once. I am amazed it has not happened many, many times, given the long days and short nights some of our clients have to endure. In this particular instance, I was sailing along, and all at once the dictation stopped. I assumed the doctor was gathering his thoughts, or as often happens, shuffling his papers to find some particular bit of information. So I waited, fingers poised over the keys, waiting to move on. And I waited... and waited. I had just about decided that he had been cut off,

when I heard… you guessed it… snoring! I sat there smiling for a while, happy that the poor fellow was finally getting a few moments of sleep, then all at once there was sputtering and fussing about, and believe it or not, he actually picked up precisely where he had left off, mid sentence, and continued his dictation as if nothing had happened.

I had another wonderful client who always dictated a joke before he started every dictation. Now this guy would be the love of every transcriptionist's heart. He also happened to be my next door neighbor, and I can definitely attest to the fact that he fit squarely into the category of "Among My Favorite Doctors." He was a well-rounded, charming, socially adept, wonderful individual, husband and father, and, incidentally, a very capable and highly respected physician. What a pleasure! Those jokes were just the icing on the cake.

Lastly, several years ago I landed a terrific account with my local county mental health clinic. It involved dictations by several staff psychiatrists, none of whom I had met, of course. Right out of the bag, the first day I put on those ear phones and took a big anticipatory breath, fingers poised, what came through into my ears? A very very bad personal vocal rendition of a Christmas carol. Now I am not at all opposed to Christmas carols. It certainly got my attention, partly because it was hardly what I had anticipated, partly because it was of extremely poor quality, but mostly because it just happened to be July! You just gotta love 'em, right? I will have to admit, it took all the starch out of me, I had a terrific laugh, and when I settled down to do the serious work at hand, I was certainly relaxed.

I continued to transcribe that physician's reports for a few years and for quite awhile I could always count on an awful rendition of some song each time he began his day's dictations, albeit that was the last Christmas carol I got from him. Sadly, after a couple of years, he abruptly stopped, and I cannot tell you how

much I missed it. I do not know if his superior put the kibosh on it or whether he ran out of songs, I never found out, and he eventually left the organization. I miss those dreadful songs. By the way, early on, I sent him an email and actually thanked him for his daily musical diversions. Do not ever overlook the fact that down in there somewhere lurks a truly sensitive soul and, like everyone else, that soul needs an "attaboy" now and then.

And so, as in every endeavor in life, medical transcription has its aggravations and irritations. Then there are those shining moments that make it all worthwhile. Our clients are human, subject to idiosyncracies and foibles, just like everyone else. I would not have it any other way.

CHAPTER 11

Some Random Thoughts

I was once told, by the physician-friend mentioned in an earlier chapter, that physicians are taught in medical school to show no emotion during a physical examination, to make no comment, make no unusual facial expression. I truly believe that. Haven't you noticed, when you are being examined, how attentive you are to the doctor's slightest hint of what he is seeing or finding? If you are apprehensive about something, you will be watching that doctor like a hawk, won't you? You will not ascertain a thing from his reaction, right? You have to wait until the examination is over, and then and only then will the doctor sit down and talk with you about his or her findings. So I do believe that my friend was telling the truth--they are taught to hide their emotions and reactions. Think about it: How would you feel if, during an examination of, say, an abscessed wound, the doctor would go "oooo, yuck," or a similar comment. Worse yet, he would say something like "Oh, no," or "Wow, that's awful." Of course, I am being a bit facetious to make my point, but it only illustrates how completely out of the question something like that would be. We never ever hear or see that kind of response from our physicians. Thank goodness!

Similarly, have you ever noticed how our clients dictate the most hilarious or outrageous incidents in their reports and never show emotion? We are sitting there thinking "Oh, no, how disgusting," or we are laughing at an incident the doctor is describing, and yet he drones on in his usual monotone, never showing the slightest reaction to what he is saying. So there is that medical school training, kicking in again. I suppose every transcriptionist has had at least one exception to that rule. I believe, in all my years, it has happened once. The doctor tried his best to maintain his decorum, but he simply could not and burst out laughing. Sure, it is terribly unprofessional, but there are rare occasions when our human instincts overpower what we have been trained to do.

"Getting into The Zone." This is just a "transcriptionist thing." Sort of a right of passage. It will take a novice some time to achieve this state, but she will know when she is there. Simply put, it is almost a form of hypnotism. You are going along, words going into your ears, words coming out through your fingertips and onto the screen. All the while you are engrossed in making your grocery list, reliving some wonderful vignette from last night's party, solving the problems in your life, or everyone else's lives. Most importantly, you definitely are not focused on what you have just typed. What a strange phenomenon, but ask any veteran transcriptionist and they will clearly understand. We call it "getting your rhythm," "getting into the zone," or "going on autopilot." It is fascinating, isn't it? It might seem that this is a careless approach to your work. It really isn't, because as you are typing, and daydreaming, when you encounter something amiss, poor grammar, a switch of appendages from right to left, an incorrect medication, you are instantly snapped back to the task at hand. Most of the time you will actually correct the error and have no memory of having done so once you complete the report. It is truly amazing. It never ceases to astound me, that I can complete an entire report and realize I had no idea what that report was about. If the last sentence or two piques my interest, I actually have to go back and re-read the report to find out what happened. This ability or talent or whatever you may call it takes time. You will know you have "arrived" as a medical transcriptionist when you finally achieve this state.

I have accused our physicians of some interesting and often outrageous habits and faux pas. We transcriptionists are guilty as well. Few cause more red faces than the unexpected consequences of our word-expansion programs. Most veteran transcriptionists use word expansion programs of one sort or another. Word-expander software is a sort of shorthand. We type in a shortened version of a word or phrase and the software expands it out to what it is intended to be. For example, I can type in "pre" and on the screen I get "PREOPERATIVE DIAGNOSIS." We love this capability, obviously, because it saves us strokes, saves us time, and at least for the independent contractor, ultimately makes us more money at the end of the day. However, there are hazards, and I am sure that every transcriptionist has a horror story to tell in this regard. In my case, several come to mind. For instance, I programmed in "fl" to replace "phlegm." I was horrified one day to discover, too late, that I had sent a letter to a very important person in Florida. You've got it. The inside as well as the outside address went to Miami, Phlegm! I assume the post office figured it out, and can only hope the recipient likewise used word expanders and understood.

More than once I have typed in the word "Inn," as in "We stopped at an inn," and it ended up saying "We stopped at an injury." That was not nearly as bad as the time I used the word "nabs," and it came out "normoactive bowel sounds." How about "mgr," and I got "murmurs, gallops and rubs." Perhaps my best

one was when I referred to "pbs," or public broadcasting station in a letter. When I proofread the letter (fortunately), what was on the screen instead of "pbs"? "Positive bowel sounds." Now that is when good proofreading is essential.

All transcriptionists realize that a large majority of their work never gets read by the physician who dictated it, in spite of the fact that when a physician signs his name at the bottom, he is verifying that everything there is accurate. This can be discouraging. Nonetheless, we have to continually remind ourselves that producing an accurate report is our job and does make a difference. Once we send off a document, we must be satisfied that we transcribed it as perfectly and accurately as possible. Then we have done our job. We must always be aware that this same report will almost certainly will be reviewed for purposes of further treatment, insurance reimbursement and legal protection. What we transcribe may be the key to what kind of care a patient receives, and even whether a patient lives or dies. Occasionally, a document even ends up in the legal system and what we have put on those pages will play a key role in a vital legal case. When we are in the midst of transcribing a document, we have no idea what its destiny will be, and we must treat each individual document as if it is the one that will make a difference somewhere down the road.

If you become a home-based transcriptionist, your fashion skills may gradually disappear.

CHAPTER 12

Independent Contractor? Acute Care Setting? Choices, Choices, Choices...
Work at Home or at the Office?

*Y*ou have taken all your classes and have learned all that you can about being a transcriptionist. You have studied anatomy, physiology, pharmacology, grammar, punctuation and business practices. You have reached that all-important place where you have some critical decisions to make. You must decide how to apply what you have learned. In some cases, in fact in many cases, your life circumstances are dictating how you pursue your career.

Many of you chose medical transcription because of the unique arrangements it offers. Some of you have young children at home, and the idea of pursuing a career away from home is not only unappealing but is impractical. You are heading in the direction you chose at the time you joined the ranks of this profession. However, some of you simply gravitated to medical transcription because you loved it. You do have choices, and this is your moment to make some important decisions.

Your choices are varied, such as working as an independent contractor at home, working for a transcription service, working in a physician's office, or working in an acute care facility. Of course, you will always have options and you can make little or big changes in your career at any time.

If you choose to work at home as an independent contractor, (IC), you have surely been warned, or at least counseled, that it is most imperative that you get your feet wet in a hospital or clinic setting. I cannot emphasize strongly enough how important this is.

Working at home has so many advantages, which I will address later, but there are disadvantages as well. As a neophyte, it can be very lonely. When you sit down, all alone, put on those headphones and strike out on that first dictation, you will feel as if you are the only human being on the planet. It is just Murphy's Law that you will run into a roadblock, an unintelligible word, or worse, a terrible dictator, within minutes of beginning. And you will panic. You listen and listen, it gets no clearer. Now what do you do? In your classes you always had someone sitting next to you to help, or you could even ask the instructor. Now, you look around and all you see is your faithful dog, comforting to have around, but not much help getting you past this problem. This will happen over and over and over again. It doesn't matter how much training you have, how many hours of dictation you have transcribed, you will run into barriers such as these… and you will be alone.

In addition to transcription challenges, you are also in charge of business operations. These can include marketing, advertising, recruiting subcontractors, negotiating contracts with clients, invoicing and bookkeeping, delivery of transcription, and maintenance of office equipment, to name only a few.

The universal advice to anyone planning on becoming an independent contractor, and working all alone, is... don't. Not for a while, at least. Get thee to a large transcription service, a clinic or hospital. Go where there are trained transcriptionists to hold your hand. Do this for as long as it takes to get completely comfortable and confident that you are ready to strike out on your own. This may take months. You may find yourself struggling alongside someone else for a year or more. Don't leave that situation until you can honestly say you are ready.

Try coming to work one day, and pretending you are home, alone. Ignore your fellow workers (let them know ahead of time), and imagine they simply are not there. You hit a stumbling block — figure it out. By yourself. Remember, that's what you are going to have to do at home.

There are ways around these dilemmas. You can call a transcriptionist buddy. You can call the office where the doctor dictated and ask the medical assistant, or ask the doctor himself. You can call a pharmacy or the appropriate department at the hospital.

As a newbie, you cannot afford to spend the time it would take to track down answers every time you encounter a bump in the road, and your resources will soon tire of constant questions. Therefore, you need to remain close to other transcriptionists in a clinic or hospital for a long time. Then, when you do strike out on your own, you will have the experience and confidence to get through most of the challenges. You will know that word, whereas you would not have had a clue months earlier. You will know how to perform the necessary detective work to find the answer you need. Most importantly, you will know you are right when you are right, (this is often overlooked, but it is an important part of the picture).

What if you follow the advice above? You know you need

some handholding and you decide to seek employment in an acute care setting or a transcription service. Be prepared to face the old Catch-22. They won't hire you because you have no experience and you cannot acquire experience because they will not hire you. Now what do you do?

This is a tough one, and I can only offer these suggestions. You are a freshly graduated student. You are that person so desired by overworked and overbooked independent contractors. Put out the word, network, make calls, contact all the independent contractors in town and offer your services. Granted, this is not ideal. You still do not have another transcriptionist sitting next to you, ready and able to help. Be up front. Let them know you are wet behind the ears and will need close supervision for awhile, but that you are eager to acquire the experience, you are thoroughly reliable, etc. They will probably be willing to invest the time to patiently answer your numerous phone calls and all the "listen-to-this" cries for help. After all, this arrangement will ultimately benefit them as well. This is where your hard work and diligence in your classes will pay off. If you were a good student, use your instructor as your best reference.

No independent contractors around who need you? Perhaps you are fortunate enough to live near a hospital that has training/mentoring programs. If you have good credentials, they will probably welcome you.

If all this fails, beg! Well, not really, but try presenting your local hospital or transcription service with a proposal. You will be willing to work for practically nothing just to gain experience. Not good enough? You will be willing to work for nothing for a specified period of time. Do whatever it takes to get your foot in the door, gain the mandatory experience, and then move on. It is a buyer's market out there these days. Hospitals are desperate for qualified transcriptionists.

A quick thought here: When you finally have several years

behind you and you are a veteran transcriptionist in whatever venue you have chosen, take time to remember how it felt when you first began. Then, pass it on. Be willing to help the next generation of struggling students. Become a mentor. It will feel very good and it will sharpen your own skills.

I had an eye-opening experience several months ago. I had not been in a hospital or clinic transcription setting since I first began transcribing over 29 years ago. I thought I remembered how it was. Boy, was I wrong. I visited a local transcription department to acquire hands-on training in a new system. The department occupied a very large room, partitioned by half-walls, making rows and rows of cubicles. It was amazing. There was constant interaction among the transcriptionists. The communication and interchange left me wide-eyed and dumbfounded. I had no idea how isolated, by comparison, I had been all these years. These transcriptionists exchanged information, made inquiries, consulted each other and conferred with one another. It was something I had not expected at all and it truly astonished me. Conversely, I am sure, had any of them been placed in the home environment where I spend my time, they would have been equally amazed.

Obviously, when comparing working at home to working in an office, one difference is the support of fellow workers, or lack thereof, depending on which avenue you choose. While working uninterrupted at home may be highly productive, there is something to be said for camaraderie, office esprit de corps, the feeling of belonging to a larger entity.

Do you enjoy getting dressed up each morning? Are you someone who cannot function unless you have "dressed the part"? If so, you should be looking for a job somewhere in the public work force. I can almost guarantee that if you become a home-based transcriptionist, your fashion skills, and unfortunately, sometimes even pride in your appearance, may

gradually disappear. It seems doubtful that you would make the effort to put on a killer outfit and then sit at your desk all alone and work. If it is important to you to dress up and look stunning every day, I do not recommend home-based transcription.

While working at home over the years, I have always made an effort to shower, put on makeup, (well, at least lipstick), comb my hair, and yes, most of the time I even put on clothes before I begin my work. My favorite outfits are loose and comfortable, casual but presentable.

Ask any home-based transcriptionist what her favorite "work outfit" is and you will get some outrageous answers, all the way from, of course, pajamas, to, yep, nothing at all. I plead guilty. I have been fortunate enough to live in very private settings, and on an occasional blistering hot day, I have been known to dispense with clothing altogether. Granted, I always keep a throw-on garment nearby, just in case the meter reader happens along (I have a dog to warn me). I know, it's not a pretty picture, but why not? It is just one of the perks of working at home.

Do you mind climbing into the car and driving some distance to your work place? Would you rather leave the car in the garage and "walk" to work — fifteen paces across the hall to your office? There is a lot to be said for this. Depending on your domestic situation, it might even make the difference between having a car or not, or having one car instead of two. There is quite a savings right there.

You may have heard that when you work from home, your time is your own. While this is sometimes true, it is not always the case. If you work at home, you can usually decide when you want to work, and to some extent, how much you want to work. Obviously, there will be some exceptions. If you have to interact frequently with your clients, you should plan your schedule around their work hours. If, on the other hand, you work for a national organization, there is usually 24-hour support available and you can work whatever hours you choose. Regardless what limitations you might have, working from home usually lends itself to a flexible schedule.

In contrast, there certainly can be a downside to working at home. One of the most difficult issues is providing coverage for sick days and vacations. As I mentioned in a prior chapter, the little story about my niece on jury duty says it all. What do we do when we are really sick? We run into the bathroom, throw up, crawl back to our desk and get back to work. No work, no pay.

Vacation time? What a dilemma! Many home-based transcriptionists have worked years without taking time off. Not only is it financially prohibitive, finding someone to fill in is a nightmare, fraught with all sorts of pitfalls. First of all, who do you know who is qualified to do your work, and who has the time? If she's that good, she probably has more work than she can handle and cannot possibly take on more. Let's say she is able to squeeze in some of your work so you can get away for a few days. The only fair thing to do is reciprocate. Down the line you are going to have to squeeze in her work for a few days so she can get away. This can be frantic and exhausting. Transcribing unfamiliar dictation is always difficult. It can take weeks, if not months, to get in stride.

Let's say you are finally planning some time away and have decided to let the work accumulate while you are gone, if that is even possible. Some doctors' offices will cooperate and work with you in that regard. Others will insist you find coverage for them. If you are able to let the work ride until you return, it takes days and sometimes weeks to catch up, all the while trying to keep up with your current work. By the time you get things back on an even keel, you most certainly are needing another vacation. It can be brutal. I have done this many times and always vow never to do it again. I always do, and it never gets any easier.

The bottom line is, getting away from work has never been easy, and probably never will be. I have tried all kinds of solutions: Take my work with me (ridiculous); find and train a neophyte just in a single account (nearly useless); turn the work over to a large transcription service (very poor results); utilize one of my "students" who is up to speed but has yet to acquire any accounts on her own (pretty tricky timing); and probably some other outlandish ideas I may have forgotten over the years. None of these solutions have been ideal.

Are you the social type or the "I want to be alone" type? If you love the peace and quiet of solitude, if working independently is what you do best, then obviously home is where you belong. However, if you need the stimulation of activity around you, if you look forward to the interaction of other people, then by all means you belong in an office.

When it comes to money, it can work both ways. As mentioned previously, working at home saves money in some ways, i.e., no transportation costs, no wardrobe to speak of, probably less money on food (a lunch time snack at home generally ends up, in the long run, being less expensive than even packing a lunch, and certainly cheaper than buying lunch out). Additionally, there is always that "home office deduction" at income tax time.

On the other hand, when you work at home, you must pay your own medical insurance and there are no other benefits. There are no 401K contributions, and, of course, there is no vacation pay or sick pay. When it comes to buying and maintaining all the necessary equipment and supplies - oh wow, you had better sit down for that one. The initial outlay is staggering (usually requiring a loan). As the years go by, you can always count on something needing to be replaced or upgraded just when you least expect it. Remember the Kauai story about trying to hook up all those wires? You don't have to move to Kauai to face that nightmare. Just look under your desk. No matter how hard you try to create order, it will always resemble spaghetti. Therefore, it is absolutely imperative that you find yourself a willing and talented friend/relative/neighbor who can decipher all that equipment you must have on hand. I am referring not only to hardware, but most certainly to software as well. There will be no technical support team to summon when you desperately need them, so you had better have one of your own. I have a transcriptionist friend who has told me if her current husband were to die or leave her, the next time around she definitely would not marry for money, she would marry for technical support!

How does it all balance out in the end? It's hard to say. There are many variables to consider, and it would not be wise to make your decision based solely on your perception of where the better money lies.

I learned a long time ago that I love the feeling of earnings directly related to the amount of work I do. I tend to be a fast worker, goal oriented, and I am clearly more intense and focused than is probably healthy for me, but that just happens to be my personality. I cannot begin to imagine how it would feel to sit in an office, furiously cranking out work, knowing that at the end of the day, I could earn the same money by kicking back and slowing rolling along. That just does not compute in my brain. Frankly, for me, that sounds painfully depressing. No wonder then I have never considered any other arrangement than the one I have. There was not enough money to persuade me to leave my home base. I am fully aware that there are equally as many people in hospitals, clinics and doctors' offices who are saying, "They could not pay me enough money to make me stay all cooped up in the house, day after day." Vive la difference!

If you are leaning toward being an independent contractor, you need to do a very thorough and honest self-assessment. Besides all the issues already mentioned, you should ask yourself the following questions: Am I a self starter? Am I motivated to work without someone looking over my shoulder? Do I have a tendency to procrastinate? Am I truly responsible and dedicated to quality? Can I make hard decisions? What do I do when faced with the choice of hunkering down to get the job done versus making excuses to do it later? Would I take my work seriously, giving the tasks at hand highest priority regardless what else is swaying me? Do I have the complete support of the rest of my family (so very important)? Do I have adequate space in my home for my office without turning my life or the lives of my family upside down?

If you are wavering on more than one of these points, perhaps you should join the ranks of office-based transcriptionists and enjoy the advantages offered by that venue. There is an abundance of work to go around, and high quality transcriptionists are in great demand in both arenas.

Perhaps this is the best place to mention a huge pet peeve of mine, and all my fellow transcriptionists, and a real concern for the industry as a whole. Turn on any television, open any magazine, listen to any radio, you will soon hear claims touting medical transcription as a career. This is all well and good, to the extent that it increases awareness of our existence; however, the sad and dangerous aspect of these ads is how misleading they are.

There are two misconceptions put forth in these ads: First of all, they imply that you can take their training, be it classes or printed material, and in six months you have magically turned into a qualified, capable and talented transcriptionist. This has done immeasurable damage to the profession, to say nothing of the disappointment and probable chaos it has caused individuals and families. You will not, I repeat not, be ready in any way in six months. If you are even fortunate enough to land an account or a job anywhere at that point, you will undoubtedly fail miserably. It

CHAPTER 12

Independent Contractor? Acute Care Setting? Choices, Choices, Choices...

is so unfair to throw someone to the sharks after only six months of training. It's not fair to the person or company that hired you. It's not fair to you!, It's not fair to an industry that is trying diligently to elevate its image.

The second misconception those ads always imply is that with a minimum of time and effort you are going to be bringing in an enormous amount of money. I love my profession, as I have said numerous times throughout this book, but it is not making me a wealthy woman, not after 26 years, and most certainly not when I first began. To suggest that by simply following their quick and easy training you will suddenly be rich, well, don't believe it. As the saying goes, if it's sounds too good to be true, it probably is. When you see or hear any of these claims, turn the page, change channels, walk away. It is grossly misleading and totally unfair to someone trying to make an informed choice about their future... Whew! I feel better.

CHAPTER 13

In Search of the Perfect Subcontractor
Just Another Way to Complicate and Aggravate Your Life

*Y*ou are a home-based transcriptionist service owner. You have paid your dues, you have been struggling at this business for years, and you have finally gathered enough clients into the fold that you are... too busy. They always told you you would reach this point. You never believed it when you were looking under every rock and in every crevice for a doctor who needed your services. Gradually word got around, you proved yourself capable, and you have a full load of work. And wouldn't you know it...you get a phone call from another physician who needs you. Now what do you do? Choices are: You turn him down (ooooh, that is hard to do, isn't it?); you decide you really can get along with three hours less sleep at night; you go into a frenzy of template and macro creations to "become more efficient;" or you start searching for a subcontractor to help you out. If you are very

fortunate, you will find the perfect one — pleasant, talented, efficient, conscientious, knowledgeable, experienced, educated. Wait a minute. If she is all of that, why doesn't she have her own clients?

Of all the trials and dark days I have muddled through in 29 years, probably the darkest (not counting those times when a major piece of equipment crashed) have been those periods when I had more work than I could handle, and went through that time-consuming, discouraging process of finding someone whose hand I did not have to hold, and whose work I could be proud to turn over to my clients. I have found no easy way to do this, no magic wand that will produce that perfect candidate, but I have learned a few tips along the way. It can be done, has been done, and you can do it.

First step? Obviously, you have to get the word out there that you are looking. Here is where your networking will come in handy. Haven't done your homework on this? Shame on you! I cannot think of any better single tool in our general armamentarium than networking. It serves so many purposes — provides backup for vacations, is your best resource for solving those nasty "What is he saying?" moments, gives you moral support that cannot be matched in any other venue and helps you through dilemmas such as these. And do not overlook the fact that it offers a perfect excuse to turn off your computer, call your compatriot, and "do lunch." So if you have some good contacts, now is the time to call on them.

Not surprisingly, those ladies in the doctors' front offices frequently have good leads. After all, they "do lunch" with their cohorts on a regular basis and no doubt we, as transcriptionists, are a source of conversation from time to time. So make the rounds of your regulars and chat it up with them, see what they might have to offer.

One of my least favorite sources is the newspaper ad. If

you have tried that, you will know why. They come out of the woodwork. You will get phone calls from people who have been court reporters and "typed lots of medical terms," or RNs who, by every right, are skilled in their fields, but who cannot write a proper sentence, or even retired physicians who need to keep their fingers in the pie and fancy this as a way to do it. Then you have your "English majors" who just know they can pick it up quickly. Frankly, if I had to pick blindly from all of these, I would try my luck with the English major. At least the English major has, or should have, grammar and composition skills and only needs to learn the medical terminology. If you have the time to help her along with that, you could very well have found your ideal subcontractor. Newspaper ads will give you choices, but you can generally assume that 99 percent of them will only take up your valuable time.

If your stars are aligned perfectly in the skies, you will stumble onto someone who is qualified, but who is just starting out (that same place you were way back when), someone who has not yet acquired a full client load, and is willing to take on some subcontract work. Granted, you will have to deal with some inexperience, but if you are very fortunate, you will have found someone with brains, common sense, solid grammar skills, and you will only have to hold her hand for a short period of time until she is comfortable with whatever client you give her. Now your only fear, and well placed at that, is that she will continue to seek her own clients and will succeed. Then guess who could be the first to go?

Here is a good one… train your own. It is doable, you know. I have trained several women over the years. Granted it was when I was younger, more ambitious, and had more energy. Yes, it was time consuming. It can be successful. I can name four lovely ladies I trained from start to finish who turned out to be a tremendous help to me, were loyal to a fault (they were always so grateful for the opportunity), who eventually went on to great

success in their own businesses. So my advice is…long before you think you might need someone, start training! The key to that is to pick your students carefully! Wiggle your way out of the quagmire of training your well-intentioned but rather dense niece, for example, the temporarily enthusiastic but flaky best friend's cousin's neighbor. It is an enormous waste of time, and truly discouraging! But, find someone who is bright, sincere, enthusiastic, will stay the course and you will have a friend, colleague and helper for life… well, at least for a very long time. And do you know what the major bonus of that is? As you teach, you will learn. You will be amazed how much you learn by teaching.

Finally, if practical, given your location, etc., contact all the teaching institutions in your area that offer transcription or terminology courses. There is often a star or two in each class capable of taking on the tasks you set forth for them, and the great thing about that is the teachers of those classes will have already screened out the less-than-ideal candidates, your work is done for you, and they will be delighted to recommend their star pupils to you.

There are undoubtedly other approaches to this dilemma, but these are my most and least favorites. So don't despair. Look at it this way. If you are in need of a helper, it must mean you have been doing something very right for a long time. Because when you get to the point where you cannot handle the workload, you are a successful self-employed transcriptionist! Congratulations and happy hunting.

CHAPTER 14

Doctors do the Darnedest Things
And You Thought This Business Would Be Boring

I have previously mentioned a few idiosyncracies of the physicians we transcriptionists deal with on a daily basis. I barely scratched the surface. When you spend several hours a day, for many years, listening to doctors speak into your ears, you are bound to collect some very interesting stories. The occasional odd quirk from one of our clients is a wonderful break in our day. Bring 'em on. These quirks bring a smile, if not an outburst of laughter. Enjoy.

Parrots and dictation do not mix, especially very vocal parrots... on the doctor's shoulder. When the doctor and the parrot both speak at once, I'm hard put to know which word to type.

That idiosyncrasy is a close cousin to the doctor who bounces his screaming baby, all the while trying to dictate. You have to give this guy credit. At least he is giving mom a break,

right?

A similar situation is the doctor who dictates at home… in the kitchen, while the wife is cleaning up the dishes. Invariably, he will dictate a key word just as the wife clangs down a pan. So you go back, again and again, trying to pick up the word, and of course, each time, it's the same thing, that darned pan. This is very common with ER dictations. I don't know if most emergency departments don't provide dictating cubicles, where they can close the door, or if the doctor simply doesn't bother to find a quiet spot for his dictations. In any case, there is nothing louder than the background of an industrious orderly cleaning up an ER room, slamming pans and basins, while two feet away the doctor is attempting to make himself heard and understood. It can make for a few blanks.

Doctors sign off in some interesting ways. I had one old fellow who always said "Okthatisallgoodbye." Every single time. There have been several "Over-and-out" types as well.

One of the funniest habits of many doctors, funny mostly because it frequently trips a transcriptionist up, (not just novices but even the old hands at the business) is when a doctor will say "periodparagraph." I have been known, as have most other transcriptionists, to spend an inordinate amount of time trying to look up a medical term that sounds like that "periodparagraph," only to eventually understand. There are times like those that you really have to laugh at yourself.

I currently have a client who is the worst "uh-uh-uh" guy I've ever encountered. They all fall victim to that to some degree, but this fellow takes the prize. Sometimes I simply entertain myself and pass the time counting how many uhs he says before moving on. As I recall, his record so far is 14. If you are in a hurry, it sure can get annoying, but most of the time I am just amazed to sit and listen to it. This is not only occasionally — sadly, this happens many, many times in every single short report. What makes it worse is that once he gets himself off the "uhs," he rips through the real dictation like a runaway train, slurring, running all the words together. As can be expected, this guy is not a favorite. Oh, to add insult to injury, he has another bad habit. He will give all the demographics as he should at the beginning of the dictation, begin the body of the report, and invariably, about six to eight sentences into the report, he will stop, say "Oh, I don't know if I gave you the information, it is Mary J-O-N-E-S, number 12345, date December 14, 2005, (gives the town we are in), 30 minutes, code number 456." Now, what do I have to do during that entire totally redundant recital, including, of course, numerous "uhs"? Of course, I sit there with my fingers poised, waiting. I have sent him polite emails, telling him that "really, it is not necessary," but he continues to do it. When every minute counts, you are trying to finish, and your income depends on how much work you can crank out in a given period of time, this habit clearly falls into the "Major Annoyance" category.

Modern dictating equipment does allow for pauses, actually very long pauses in most cases. Most doctors believe that they must make a sound of some kind every second or they will be disconnected. This is more prevalent than you might imagine. While they are looking up something among their papers, (remember the shuffling papers?) they keep talking. They tend to say about the same thing, usually something like "holding, holding, holding, holding," or "pausing for a moment, pausing for a moment," or sometimes "looking, looking, looking, still looking, still looking." Of course, the standard "looking for something, looking for something" is a favorite. They will continue to repeat these mantras endlessly, until they are ready to continue their primary dictation. It's a shame they can't get the concept of a pause, it would save them so much stress. Now here is a novel idea: push the pause button. I could probably count on one hand the number of doctors over the years who ever used the pause button. It never ceases to amaze me that these brilliant people

made it through eight years or more of complex learning, and still cannot get it in their heads that when they are not speaking, they can push the pause button. It is exactly what it says, it allows you to pause. Again, it gives us a little diversion in our day.

Speaking of a brilliant doctor "not getting something," my all-time favorite is a doctor who was, and still is, truly one of the most outstanding in his particular specialty; one who was able to develop his fledgling practice into an enormously successful business in just a few years, who is well known in his field, one who makes more money in a week than I will see in a year, and who is known everywhere to have nearly magic fingers when he performs surgery. He has side businesses galore, ranches, wine connections — you name it.

Several years ago, I had been trying for many months, working with and through his vast office staff, to get him to finally come into the modern age with his computer (i.e. allow me to quit sending his voluminous transcriptions back to him in hard copy, by snail mail). Can you believe it? He only needed to hook up a modem to his computer so I could use the connection to transfer all his files back to him. I was getting nowhere with the office staff, so one day I was in his town (this was one of my long distance accounts). I managed to grab him between surgical cases, sat him down, looked him in the eye and said, "Doctor, you just have to get a modem so we can simplify and speed up our communication." His answer? "Look around here, Sara, where on earth would I put a modem?" I kid you not, this brilliant, successful doctor actually said that to me. Needless to say, it took me awhile to close my dropped jaw, quit staring at him in utter disbelief, suppress a smile, and try to salvage the moment by gently and kindly explaining to him that a modem is about as big as a playing card and fits inside the computer. Within a month we had our modem in place. Lest you think I am telling tales out of school, and this fellow would be highly offended that I have included this little incident in my book, I can assure you, he will be the one to laugh loudest when he reads this. And I will see that he has a copy of the book. He loves to laugh at himself, just one of the appealing character traits that makes him so special. Way to go, Doc!

Remember that belching, apple-eating doctor who turned out to be so adorable? I have a sweet little followup story on him. Did I mention that he was single? Need I say that there was a very long line of hopeful single women always waiting in the wings for their chance with our cutie? Well, one of them finally broke through the throngs and actually landed this prize. They eventually were married, and very soon after the honeymoon he returned to work and one of my fellow transcriptionists happened to be doing some of his dictation. He completed his work and supposedly hung up the dictating phone. As fate would have it, the phone didn't hang up properly. Our boy proceeded to pick up another phone nearby and he called his new bride. You guessed it, a long conversation ensued, and my friend was privy to the entire performance! Every "poochie-poo" and "honey-buns," along with some occasional x-rated remarks. Now what was my friend supposed to do, hang up? Would you have hung up?

I have experienced the other side of that coin a couple of times, one being a conversation between a doctor and his office manager/wife. The good wife was whispering to her husband that his breath was less than stellar and he needed to do something about it. I felt like such an intruder in that very private exchange between husband and wife, but what was I to do? The other time was quite a bit more interesting than that. This doctor was doing some dictating at home and failed to turn off his dictating machine. I was entertained for approximately 15 minutes with a vociferous, less-than-loving exchange between the doctor and his wife. I don't remember the subject of the argument now (I would venture to guess they don't either), but I can assure you they were quite angry and neither one was backing down. I certainly had a front row seat to the other side of these two people who always presented such loving and calm personas in the office. In situations like this, a transcriptionist truly does have to listen through whatever she is hearing, regardless how personal it is. You never know when the doctor will pick up and continue his dictation, and it would be irresponsible to miss any important dictation. Anyway, what a diversion in an otherwise routine day.

So never become complacent. About the time you think you have heard it all, something will come along that wakes you up and makes you realize yet again what an interesting business this can be.

CHAPTER 15

The Dreaded QA (Quality Assurance)
I Knew I Didn't Want to Come to Work Today

*W*hen I see those QA sheets coming off the fax machine, my day is instantly altered. To the initiated, the subject of QA can create as much anxiety and apprehension as a letter from the IRS. To the uninitiated, QA stands for Quality Assurance. In a clinic or hospital setting, there is usually one person designated as Quality Control. She keeps her eye on your work, she corrects, suggests, guides and generally assures that the department will produce... well... quality work.

There are many ways to set up quality control, but primarily, a good quality control person can do her job without alienating every employee in the department. No doubt about it, it is just downright tough to take criticism. The harder you try, the more difficult it is to be told your work is not up to par. However, I believe that it is definitely a 50/50 proposition. It is imperative that the QA individual uses every means at her disposal to present her criticism in a way that is not offensive, insulting or degrading, presenting it with an attitude of "we're a team and let's make sure we clear up a few things so we can present an excellent product." This is a very difficult task.

I have never been a true QA person, but I have certainly done my share of editing, correcting and teaching in my time. As I said in an earlier chapter, I have trained several wonderful ladies as medical transcriptionists, and this involved occasionally playing the QA role. I tried my best to never offend my students, but I don't fool myself. I'm sure there were several times when my students walked away with their hard work in their hands, red pencil marks all over the pages, with some choice words under their breath for me. I don't blame them a bit, it's hard to take. I feel a great deal of empathy for the QA manager. She will never win any popularity contests, no matter how diplomatic she is. Nevertheless, it is her job, and if she does her best to be respectful, you can ask for no more than that.

What about the other "50" in that 50/50 deal, the transcriptionist on the receiving end of all that criticism? Is it tough to take? You bet it is! I think the key lesson to learn here is to step back, remind yourself what the real goal is, consider it always a learning process, and don't kill the messenger! She is simply doing what she was hired to do. Instead, thank her. Then crawl back into your little work space, start perusing the pages with the red marks all over them, and figure out what you can learn from it and how you can improve. This can take the hard edges off those resentful feelings that keep wanting to creep in. Make a list of everything that needs to be changed or corrected, stick it up on the side of your screen (along with the 200 other stickies you already have there), and move on. She will have done her job and you will have done yours, and everyone will benefit. End of subject. However, if you do not understand something or you don't agree, do not hesitate to take it up again with the QA individual. Do not do it in a way that seems like "you are wrong" or "I don't agree with you," maybe say something like "I'm not really clear on what you mean by this, could you explain it to me in another way?" An accusatory attitude gets you nowhere, while obvious desire to really understand and learn from your mistakes will go a long way.

Imagine an office in a ratty old 10-foot camper trailer parked alongside that RV.

CHAPTER 16

Transcription on Wheels
The Other Side of the Aforementioned Tropical Odyssey

A few chapters back I told of our incredible adventure in Kauai; a year of living and working in a beautiful condo, right on the ocean, watching the whales and dolphins as I hammered out my daily reports. Lest anyone let envy get the best of them, I am going to even the playing field and share with you another adventure, the opposite end of the spectrum, a saga that will leave no one with a case of envy.

Herein lies our other adventure, but this time no condo, no ocean, no tropical breezes. Visualize a 23-foot RV. It gets even better. Imagine an office in a ratty old 10-foot camper trailer parked alongside that RV.

My husband and I, and our daughter, bought five acres deep in the woods in the Sierra Nevada Mountains in Northern California. She has moved into the house and we are building a granny unit on the property. Yes, we are currently living in that

23-foot RV while our home is being built, and I am conducting my business out of the 10-foot camper trailer parked alongside. Doesn't that sound special?

Picture this — I walk out of the RV in the wee hours of the morning (my inner clock runs on a very strange schedule). It is pitch black and chilly outside. I step two or three paces and jerk open the rickety door of my "office." With my tiny flashlight I stretch and reach, plugging in my haphazardly hung little light. Oops, have to be careful — don't want to hit my head — there is a shelf full of machines and temporarily discarded accouterments of my business precariously situated in front of and just at about eye level (I believe at one time it served as a bunk bed, but has definitely taken on a new roll).

I untangle my ergonomic chair (inappropriate for such a small space, but something I insisted on) from the desk to my immediate right, carefully sit down and try to navigate amongst wires and cords, consoles and foot pedals, the few inches into position to begin my day. There are cords dangling inches from my nose, cords draping around the monitor, and my mouse pad is nearly hidden beneath a collection of notepads, pens, blank printer paper, and whatever else was leftover from the night before. Do not misunderstand. Under normal circumstances I am Miss Neat and Organized. This arrangement, however, has bested me. I give up. I try to find the foot pedal — again a maze of wires fights my foot as I reach and feel for the pedal. I mention here, for further clarification, that there are seven — yes seven! — phone lines feeding into that small space and interconnected among various machines and small gadgets, most of which are a mystery to me, being technically challenged as I am.

Why seven phone lines, you ask? Let me explain. My business requires a private/business line, a dedicated line to the fax machine, the Internet line, three rotating lines to my dictating machine, and one line to the aforementioned C-phone. There is even an unseen eighth line, an 800 line that somehow piggybacks in on one of the other lines. I think the phone company suspects us of running a bookie joint.

A considerable portion of my day is spent "looking for things." Things that should be in THAT drawer, things that I know I put RIGHT THERE yesterday, things that are hidden beneath things that are underneath other things that are buried behind still other things. Again, do not accuse me of being disorganized. There simply is no way to organize such an accumulation of papers, documents, mail, normal desk equipment, and the myriad other bits of flotsam and jetsam that one typically keeps carefully stowed away in convenient cubbyholes. There just too many cubbies and too few holes. Remember, it is crowded in there — drawers that normally open to reveal their contents cannot be opened because there is yet something else right across the way, fighting for space. Do not forget that the trailer lacks, shall we say, symmetry? A slight sag here, a twist there. If a cupboard door actually opens at all, it only offers an intriguing peak at what is or might be inside.

Let us talk about weather. This saga began during the dead of winter, with snow sometimes so deep we could barely get our car in and out. We are talking cold. Enter a floor heater to add to the mix of things for which there was no room. Constant monitoring of the dials barely prevented either a serious chill or near roasting. This was not a modern heater, by any stretch of the imagination. Then came the rains and as luck would have it, the total rainfall for this season was twice normal — 94 inches. Do old rickety trailers have leaks? What do you think?

We survived that weather challenge, as well as the sweltering summer, with humidity nearly unknown in these parts. I would walk into my "office" and run right into an oven. But never fear — the huge floor fan to the rescue, adding yet another element to walk over and around. I would try to position

it such that it offered relief, yet allowed me to back my chair up more than three inches, and stand up without hitting my head for the hundredth time on that bunk bed just inches above my computer. There is serious concern for the equipment in such hot weather, so we added still another small fan, attaching it to the computer table. That's right — inches from my left knee. I tried to focus. I could not stand up because I would hit my head on the bunk bed, I could not move my left knee because it would run into a fan. I could not back up because I would knock over the raucously loud and oversized fan behind me. I could not move my right leg because it would become so entangled in wires that I would have to call for help to be extricated. There were papers and notebooks, and other important parts of my work to my right, and telephones to my left. Good grief!

As this book goes to press, the entire adventure is unfolding. We have spent a year under these living and working conditions, so we are obviously in our second winter, and the end is barely in sight. It is truly a test of our adaptability and patience, along with a good dose of ingenuity. It takes a real flight of imagination to remember that I am a professional, a medical language specialist, and have obligations and ties to the outside world, while trying to function in an ambiance that is anything but professional. Can I continue to pull it off? I must. It will not be the first time I have been faced with a challenge in my work. I think it all comes down to attitude, and I did my best to prepare myself for this strange voyage. It is just another chapter in this chronicle of my life and my work. It always has been a little out of the ordinary and it does not appear to be turning dull anytime soon. Stay tuned.

CHAPTER 17

Is the End of the Road in Sight?
The Engine is Slowing Down

*R*etirement — is it really the panacea it is cracked up to be? Is it the perfect reward for your many years of work and struggle? Some people will tell you that retiring is the worst thing you can do to body, mind and soul. It is that daily challenge of an active work experience that keeps you alive and healthy and vital. Tell that to the transcriptionist who has struggled for years and years and wants nothing more than to hang up the earphones, put her feet up on her computer table, breathe a huge sigh of relief and do... and do...?

Of course, you can have plans and goals, adventures that were unthinkable when those offices were waiting impatiently for your next delivery. Cold turkey retirement is not always possible or even desirable. I would guess that a large majority of transcriptionists would find an abrupt cessation of income not only unpleasant but probably completely impossible. I have faced that dilemma myself. There is an irony here. I want to travel but do not have time because of my work. Yet if I quit work to travel, I will not have the financial resources to afford the travel. What a nasty dilemma.

After numerous nights staring into the dark, trying desperately to solve this problem, I hit on a very good solution, at least in my specific circumstances. If I could figure out a way to work one month, and then take off a month, I would have the best of both worlds: one month pretending I was retired, the next month working like a demon making money to pay for the "retired" months.

It seemed like it should work, and basically it has worked. However, in reality, it took almost a year, and several missteps and start-overs, to implement it. Fortunately, when I was ready to try my idea, I had only three major clients. One was a large county mental health clinic and there was no question about their needs. Forty-eight hour turnaround, five days a week, 52 weeks a year.

My answer to that was find someone who wanted the same thing I wanted: one month on, one month off. After a couple of tries I finally found not only an excellent transcriptionist, but someone who was wildly enthusiastic about the idea. After all, it provided her the same advantages it gave to me. The client needed a little persuasion and a lot of convincing, but that eventually worked out.

My second account, two plastic surgeons, did mostly operative reports. Since they were not the best at staying current with their dictation, delays in turnaround time were seldom a problem. Ultimately they agreed to a plan whereby they would continue to dictate their reports whenever it was convenient for them, and I would be allowed to let them accumulate during my month off, then catch up the following month. This came with one caveat: if, at any time, during either month, they had a stat (urgent) report, I, or someone else, would be available, or on call, to transcribe it immediately. Another part of the puzzle was solved.

My last account consisted of two large hospital emergency departments. I was only one of many transcriptionists who tapped into their main system and took work off only as we wanted or were able to. They had no problem accommodating my plan. I simply would not take any work during my month off. Last part of the puzzle solved. Just like our seemingly foolish plans to move to Kauai several years ago, this fit equally into the "Where there is a will, there is a way" philosophy. It is working well, so far. Everyone seems satisfied with the arrangement.

I have discovered one thing about myself, though. Even on my "months off," I am drawn to that computer more often than I care to admit. When I have an idle moment, do I read a book? Do I take a walk? Do I go shopping? Nooooo. I return to that familiar chair, pick up the headphones and plunge back into work. I am not proud of it. I am sure a psychiatrist would have a field day with this one. However, as I try to explain to my husband, the big difference is that I am doing it because I want to, not because I have to. When I am driving around town running errands, I do not have that feeling that I need to get home, that work is accumulating and that it must be done. When it hits me that there is no work waiting, and that I can actually choose not to work, without consequences, now that feels like retirement! Oh my, does that feel good.

I think part of the dilemma I face (and I would venture to guess I am not alone), is that for 29 years I have defined who I am by what I do. What I do is transcribe medical reports. I am a medical transcriptionist, a medical language specialist. If I retire, I will have to find a new identity, learn to see myself as something other than what I do to make a living. That is not going to be easy. I suppose the interim step will be to identify myself as a retired transcriptionist, and it might take the edge off a cold-turkey

approach.

Maybe I am not so obsessed with it after all. Maybe one of these days I really will hang up my earphones for good. I will not deceive myself into thinking it is just going to happen on its own. I will always have the financial issues to work out, and I suppose I will never lose the urge to sit down at the computer and become absorbed once again in my wonderful world of medicine. I know there is another world out there, beckoning to me, a world that will offer me all sorts of delights. All I have to do is take that big step away from the only routine I have known for over 29 years.

I stated at the beginning of this book that I intended to appeal to three groups of readers: the seasoned, experienced transcriptionist who I hoped would find a lot of "Oh, yeah, been there's" in these pages; that collection of wannabes who had been toying with the notion of taking on this unique profession; and that diverse bunch who just happened upon the book, were curious, started thumbing through the pages and could not put it down. My wish is that I have succeeded in all three categories. If I have lightened a transcriptionist's day, if I have caused someone's casual interest in transcription to blossom or if I have simply entertained the curious reader, then my goal, my purpose, my wish has been fulfilled.

CHAPTER 18

The Last Mile

I am finally nearing the last bend in the road on this long journey of medical transcription. I have often been asked if I am happy I made this my life career. The answer--without a doubt! There are many people who cannot imagine devoting 29 years to the search for words or the pursuit of a perfect medical report. I have no logical argument for them. If they have to ask why, I can never make them understand. I guess it was just right for me. Sure, I have had a few bad days when I have questioned my decision and my choice. All in all, I have no regrets. Throughout the years, the choices I made when I hit those life-changing forks in the road prepared me for the next milestone, and eventually influenced the direction my life would take, shaping my world in profound ways. My propensity for and love of all things medical pointed me in this general direction and I simply did what came naturally.

Luckily, it was a good fit and a great journey. It is not for

everyone, but it worked for me. Very soon now, I think I will pull over to the side of the road and see if I can morph into a spectator, watching in amazement (and a little envy) the new paths this fascinating business I have loved for so long will take. I hope I am ready — it has been a super ride.

APPENDIX A

Where is the Industry Headed?
The Rapid Shift in the World of Transcription

L ook quickly. The world of medical transcription as we have always known it is rapidly changing. Indeed, even the name of the organization of medical transcriptionists, AAMT, or American Association for Medical Transcription, has recently changed. Because of the rapidly changing role of the transcriptionist, there is a need to redefine who we are. We will soon be the Association for Healthcare Documentation Integrity, or AHDI.

SPEECH RECOGNITION

New technology, such as speech recognition and electronic templates, is moving us into the arena of editing rather than transcribing.

Speech recognition technology (SRT) mandates that our editing skills rise to the forefront. Absolute accuracy in medical reports still requires the human element, and medical transcriptionists are well trained to meet this requirement.

The theory of SRT has been lurking in the wings for many years, but practical implementation has been occurring slowly — until recently. It is now being perfected at a rapid rate, and physicians are beginning to give it a try. Enough are succeeding to make a significant impact on the transcription industry.

As suspected from the start, it still appears that SRT will not stand alone; the end product is definitely not accurate enough to be used as a definitive record in any patient's chart. It is clear that documents produced by SRT will always need to be edited.

One thing that transcriptionists have always been trained to do — and indeed do very well — is edit what doctors dictate. The finest doctors can be the worst dictators. Thus, the role of transcriptionists includes editing and improving dictation. This talent or expertise will become even more crucial as SRT advances.

Editing in the future may become two-fold. Some transcriptionists may find themselves editing voice dictation, while others will be editing documents produced by SRT. When a first-class transcriptionist finishes a report, the physician reads what he thought he dictated and prides himself on being the finest grammarian in town. How little he realizes what the transcriptionist went through to make this document so pristine. The rule of thumb is always to edit but never change the meaning. Herein lies the challenge.

I have transcribed reports that bear almost no resemblance to what was dictated. Don't misunderstand--I changed nothing in the way of meaning or intent, but I had to jump through all kinds of hoops, do somersaults and hand-springs all over that dictation to make it into an understandable, cohesive, logical and readable document. I corrected grammar, I completed sentences, I moved whole paragraphs up and down and around, I switched sentences from here to there, I corrected obvious errors when the right leg suddenly became the left, or when "he" magically became "she." It was endless. The amazing thing is that the dictating doctor actually believed he dictated it this way. Oh, well, just doin' my job, as they say.

Editing has always been part of our job. In the future, it will be our job. Our future most certainly lies in the field of editing as opposed to primary direct transcription. As SRT becomes more prevalent, the need for transcriptionists to hone their editing skills becomes imperative. We will be there, trained and ready to lend a hand.

OFFSHORE OUTSOURCING

These are practically dirty words in many professions, none more so than medical transcription. As many of our co-workers lose their jobs to offshore transcription services, the need to be highly competitive in the market is more critical than ever. Our task is to give the highest quality, the fastest turnaround, at the lowest possible cost. This will require implementation of advanced technology. With this in mind, SRT becomes a vital part of our future, and may be the technology that eventually keeps transcription onshore. This is a significant new trend for our profession. Keep your eye on this one.

As in every aspect of business and, indeed, our personal lives, technology has stepped in and forced such tremendous changes in how we do things, one can never become complacent. I urge you to make it a high priority. Read, study, become informed, network, reach out, and avail yourself of whatever is offered to stay current with industry trends. Take advantage of all the bells and whistles you can get your hands on. While this may seem scary, it can also be exhilarating to leap forward and be a cog in the wheel of technical evolution.

Change is happening. Our little niche in the grand scheme

of the medical world has exploded in the last few years. We are finally recognized within the medical community as a force to be reckoned with, a vital player in the field of medicine.

This transition has occurred for several reasons. One is the massive volume of documentation now required by government legislation related to patient care, confidentiality and privacy, i.e., the infamous HIPAA rules. Another factor stems from illegible, handwritten patient records, creating patient safety concerns. This is being monitored by regulatory bodies.

Finally, AAMT/AHDI has elevated the role of medical transcriptionists in the health care field by standardizing processes and raising the bar for excellence, thus promoting credibility in the professional world.

We are still a mystery to many people, but the world is beginning to appreciate our contributions to quality health care. If you eliminate medical transcription, the entire fabric of medicine will crumble. We most certainly are not the typists in the basement anymore. Along with this gradually recognized and acknowledged status must come the responsibility to generate what is needed to fulfill that vital role.

AAMT has worked diligently for many years to bring us to where we are. We have merely scratched the surface. There is so much more to do. As with any lofty goal, good people are needed to implement this vision. AAMT has accepted the challenge, staffed itself with good people, and is making huge strides in moving us out of the basement and into the higher echelons of medicine where we have always belonged. We are the glue that holds together all the elements of patient health documentation.

Once again, stay informed, do whatever is necessary to remain at the pinnacle of this profession. Make the changes work for you, not against you.

APPENDIX B

The Sanctum Sanctorum...
A Look Behind the Secret Doors

*A*s I stated in the Introduction, I ended up in this career by way of a small side street — my few years in the surgical suite — that eventually did lead me to transcription. Make no mistake--transcription was my niche, but I will always hold a soft spot in my soul for those years in Surgery. There is no doubt that what goes on behind those closed doors is intriguing. For patients lying horizontal on a gurney, it is not a fair representation, because it looks so very different. Yet it still holds a fascination, and to some of us slightly twisted people, it goes way beyond simply fascination — it is a love affair.

Curiosity runs rampant, and I will argue that that curiosity is well placed and appropriate. Even if you are terrified of all things surgical, what goes on behind those mysterious doors at least draws questions and interest, simply because you are not allowed in there. It had always been so with me. I will even

confess that after a good dose of exposure to that world, and many years since, the surgery suite still beckons to me like a Lorelei. Let me attempt to paint a picture for you, a portrait of that world few people ever see.

Driving through the nearly empty streets in the pre-dawn coolness — this was the way my day would begin. It's important to understand that solitude, the quiet, peaceful trip through the streets to the hospital, because once I would arrive, walk through the hushed, dim back corridors of the hospital and pass through the doors into the surgery suite, the instant contrast told the whole story. I would plunge into a totally different world. Bright lights, people everywhere, such scurrying about, each person intent upon his own tasks. Compared to the soft, silent world I left behind, the noise level would be startling — clanging equipment and instruments being prepared for the first cases, people communicating in loud, insistent voices, phones ringing, sometimes as many as four phones going at once, people swishing by in their scrub clothes and booties, a cacophony of clamor and sound. I absolutely loved it.

I would always get a tremendous adrenaline rush as I came through those magical doors. In an instant I became part of that unique world. I would go into the lounge, change into my scrubs (green pants and tunic top, or nondescript dress, plus bonnet and booties), grab a few bites of a Danish that was always there for us, take a big breath and push through another door into the thick of the activity. My mind would kick into high gear, I would assess the entire situation, usually get an update from the supervisor, take my place at my desk, which was the hub of the activity, and my day in Surgery would commence. What a rush! Phones would be ringing, requests would be flying, "Call the lab and tell them we need one unit of 0 positive blood," "Has the orderly gone to pick up the 7:00 yet?" "Call the floor and tell them we're on our way to pick up their patient." "Hasn't Dr. Smith arrived yet?" "What happened to the Mayo tray in Room 3?" "Call

Dr. Jones and get him here now, his patient is waiting," "I need more laps in the cysto room," "Page Dr. Brown, I think he's in the cafeteria, tell him we need him in 5 minutes." All the time there would be a constant movement of orderlies, RNs and technicians. Surgeons would be lined up at the sinks, scrubbing and chatting with each other. Gurneys would be rolled in, moved around, lined up. Whack, and the double doors would open… I can still hear that familiar sound. You never knew what or who would charge through those doors… doctors wanting their case to get started now, patients being cautiously rolled in on gurneys, other staff members checking, following up, supervising, pharmacists dropping off medications, last minute supplies.

I would always shut out all the turmoil around me and spend about three minutes getting the broad picture… who was here, who was not here, which rooms were set up, which rooms were still in process, which doctors were in the waiting room, who was already scrubbing, and which ones needed to be tracked down. It was vital to always keep that broad picture. This was not a job for someone who was not able to multitask, that's for sure! Once those first cases were tucked away into their respective rooms and the initial chaos subsided, everyone began to relax. Chit-chat could be heard up and down the halls, laughter, catching up on little details. Make no mistake about it, these were professionals, and they were always on guard, alert, attentive. No one works in Surgery who cannot constantly keep their priorities in place, that being the welfare and comfort of the patients.

A day seldom went by that something didn't occur that was more than just mildly interesting. Around my desk was a high counter, ideal for stacking things and for leaning on. I hadn't been there very long when one day I looked up from the work at my desk. There was a large cloth-wrapped object sitting on the counter. Out of curiosity, I flipped open the cloth, only to find myself staring at a lower appendage, complete with knee, ankle and foot. My reaction was exemplary… I was so proud…

"Shouldn't someone be taking this little package over to Pathology?" I calmly asked. I quickly sat back down, dropped my head and commenced with my bookwork. No one would ever know that my heart was nearly beating out of my chest. I had passed the first test. To this day I don't know if it was just my official initiation, and I was being tested. I will say that I never again encountered an entire lower extremity on my desk. Oh, there certainly were some mighty interesting items that were laid up there, appendices, fingers, gallbladders, eyeballs, but they never rose to the level of that leg and foot.

When emergencies started streaming in, and they always seemed to arrive in clusters, there would be times when every able-bodied employee was called into action in some capacity. One time I was urgently called into the operating room right next to my desk. I dropped what I was doing and rushed in. They just needed a couple of extra hands… there were more tasks than the available staff could handle. A frail little old lady was on the gurney, and they were preparing to transfer her to the operating table. My job was simply to hold the little lady's lower arm and hand while they moved her over to the table. No problem. I gently took hold of that arm, only to realize that I was holding bare arm bones. Oh, well, just part of the team.

There were occasionally things that happened that probably would not win points for best judgement. After all, this is a high-pressure setting, things move very quickly, and even though everyone worked diligently to prevent any untoward events, they did happen. We had one anesthesiologist, a true character of the first rank. It just so happened he was also the best of the bunch. Had I needed surgery, I would have demanded he be my anesthesiologist. However, he did have an irreverent streak in him. He had one favorite routine as he was waking up his patients. He would say to them, "Wake up, Dear, you didn't make it. You are in heaven and this is God speaking." Now before you gasp in horror, I want to make it very clear that he was always meticulous in his timing. He never ever said that if there was the slightest chance the patient was actually awake enough to hear it. He did it primarily for the benefit of the surgical team and simply because he had that kind of twisted humor. Sure it was crude, but it always broke the tension and never failed to make me chuckle, in spite of its inappropriateness. That kind of atmosphere often reminded me of the famous MASH series, irreverent, on the edge. Clearly, there were things said that probably, in a perfect world, should not have been said, but surgery is a very tense arena, and sometimes a little ice breaker is appropriate. I again reiterate, the patient's total well-being and comfort were always paramount for the entire team, doctors and hospital staff alike.

In spite of monumental efforts at all times, mistakes are made. There are checks and double checks, but out of many hundreds of cases, the law of averages will catch up with you. In the outside world, what would simply be a small error, in a surgical setting can have the most dire consequences. I was working at a large hospital, filling in for a vacationing surgical secretary. One day, everything was rolling along exactly as it should, everyone doing their respective jobs and all the patients were being processed through, one at a time. All at once I noticed complete silence in the suite, you could have cut the tension with a knife. I quickly put together the picture. A nurse, responsible for putting her patient on the operating table and preparing him for his procedure, had been doing her job just as she was supposed to do. She picked up her patient, took him into the operating room, transferred him to the table, made sure all the instruments and equipment specific to his case were ready to go, that the team was assembled. But just as they were ready to begin the surgery, somehow, (I never did find out how) it was discovered the nurse had brought in the wrong patient. The procedure in that room was supposed to be a leg amputation. She had brought in the appendectomy patient instead. The leg amputee was still waiting in the hall. The nurse simply walked out, went into the lounge,

changed into her street clothes and left the building. I don't know how long it was before she was able to return to work.

I was certainly not exempt from errors, although fortunately mine were of less importance. I once pulled a blunder that certainly caused raised eyebrows. Luckily, it was more hilarious than anything else. It definitely didn't cause any danger to a patient, but I was extremely embarrassed. Each day I would type up a surgery schedule for the following day. It included time of surgery, surgery procedure, and many other details, including, of course, the patient's name and age. This surgery schedule would then be distributed in the afternoon to all the hospital departments and it became the bible of scheduling for everyone the following day. This particular day I made a tiny (?) error. I typed in an 89-year-old male patient's name and next to it, for the procedure, I typed in HYSTERECTOMY. Unfortunately, the schedule was distributed throughout the hospital before I caught my error. Needless to say, phone calls flew back and forth, and it took quite awhile for me to live that one down.

Confidentiality is of such importance and is constantly drummed into all hospital employees' heads. I had always prided myself on strictly adhering to the confidentiality rules... until one day I slipped. It didn't result in anything more than a reprimand, but I sure learned my lesson. I was doing transcription on the side for an ophthalmologist. One day I typed a report for a very famous ice skater at the time. That same day I was having lunch in the cafeteria and decided to do a little name dropping and mentioned to my table mates that I had typed this report, and I mentioned the name of the patient. Needless to say, within a day or two, I was called into the ophthalmologist's office and kindly but firmly reprimanded. It seems that particular patient, the ice skater, had been sitting at the next table in the cafeteria and had overheard my remarks. Well, I was properly horrified, chagrined, and I learned my lesson big time.

Drama in the surgery suite doesn't always just happen on television. I was again substituting in a large hospital when an emergency case came through the doors. There had been a shooting nearby. It was a multiple shooting, and as I recall it was associated somehow with gang activity. One of the victims who had been shot was brought to our facility. He was quickly put in an operating room, as he needed immediate surgical intervention. A couple of detectives were just outside, not appropriately dressed in scrubs, so they were only allowed to come in just so far. However, they needed information from this fellow on the operating table and the poor guy was about to die. I somehow got dragged into the whole drama, probably because I was the only one available at the moment who wasn't needed in some other capacity. So the drama played out like this: The detectives would give me a question to ask this patient. I would run into the operating room and repeat the question to the patient. He would whisper the answer. He was so weak, I had to get my ear right down against his mouth to hear. I would then run back out and give the answer to the detectives, and the whole scene would be repeated, until the anesthesiologist finally called a halt to it and got down to the business of anesthetizing his patient. Just like the stuff in the movies.

We had several famous people come through our hospital. It was a small, out-of-the-way facility, and ideal for some of the recognizable movie stars to "hide." There was one, and how I wish I could give the name, but of course cannot (confidentiality again), who was there for several weeks "drying out." An entire hall was cordoned off, with guards at each end. It was strange, walking by day after day, seeing those guards, knowing who was there. All I could say was about what I am saying here, "There is a verrry famous person in our hospital right now, but I can't tell you who it is." Darn. I so wanted to be a name dropper.

I save my very best story for last. Again, I cannot mention

the name, but sadly, he just recently passed away. He was in our hospital for, of all things, a sigmoidoscopy. Now about everyone knows that a sigmoidoscopy is not something you look forward to with great excitement and thrilling anticipation, but we all go through it, usually in our doctor's office. This fellow, for whatever reason, (coward?) scheduled his procedure in the hospital, our hospital, under general anesthesia. It required the full workup a few days prior to surgery consisting of x-rays, EKG, lab work, the entire process. Just as a side note, the day following that workup, the x-ray technician received a bouquet of flowers from him. Wow. Lucky lady.

On the day of surgery, we all went to great lengths to appear nonchalant, but I would bet my lunch that there was not a woman in that surgery suite whose heart was not beating at double speed, including mine. Surgery went without incident and our guy was wheeled into the recovery room. After a few minutes, I couldn't stand it any longer and casually sauntered down to the recovery room to see how things were going. Now keep in mind, patients in recovery rooms react in many different ways, but most are either quiet, miserable, vomiting, sleeping, moaning or, in some cases, crying out so loud they can be heard all the way through the halls. So what was our famous fellow doing? Acting like a drunken sailor! He was hilarious! He already had a pretty thick southern drawl and that was accentuated to about double.

The recovery room nurses asked me if I wanted to go over and talk to him. Well now, what would you expect me to say? Wouldn't you have done it??? So I walked over to his gurney, looked down at him, and he looked up at me (I have to mention here, this was a very good looking guy, and unlike 99% of recovery room patients who always look like they have just been dragged behind a truck, this fellow was still as handsome as ever). I will never forget the first words he spoke to me in his familiar southern drawl, "Well, ain't you just the purtiest little thing I've

ever seen?" I thought the recovery room nurses would fall on the floor. Of course, my face turned beet red.

The nurses encouraged me to continue talking to him, try to wake him up. I honestly do not know what all I said, probably very little that made a bit of sense. Needless to say, I was shaken up. But I did get a damp washcloth and stroked (oh, doesn't that sound lovely?) his forehead, brushing his hair back. Then he said his lips were so dry. We couldn't have that, could we? The nurses gave me some Vaseline and I commenced rubbing this on his lips. What happened next will be forever seared in my memory. He took my hand, put my finger in his mouth and sucked on my finger. OK, I admit to a brief swoon, but then even I was laughing, and the nurses were out of control. I have to admit, at that point I have no idea what conversation ensued. Except that he did ask me if I would come to his room later. Need I tell anyone what my answer to that was?

Finally, it was time to take him to his room and I definitely needed a break. A quick epilogue: He had barely had time to get to his room, and the story of my encounter, finger sucking and all, was all over that hospital. I was in the halls not 15 minutes later and I hardly passed a person who had not heard the story. It was as if someone had jumped on the intercom and made an announcement in great detail to the entire hospital. And, yes, I did go to his room later, (of course I did). He was out like a light, mouth wide open, snoring, looking like the most ordinary middle-aged man you would ever NOT care about seeing. It was a good thing, I believe. Put me squarely back into reality and the entire incident immediately simply transcended into the legend that I will never forget. End of story.

So there is a small glimpse of the world behind the doors that say Do Not Enter. But I was privileged. I entered those doors day after day. It was hard work, it was most definitely exciting work, I was part of a special, unique team, and I just loved it.

This probably begs the question… if I loved it so much, why did I quit? First of all, I had, in the interim, discovered transcription and felt drawn to it. At that particular time in my life, my husband had terminal cancer and I was needed at home. Setting up a home office and pursuing the transcription route just seemed to be the right thing to do. However, I certainly cannot deny the fact that I have never really purged my system of that longing to join those special people in surgery.

REFERENCES

MY LEGS... THEY GOTTA MOVE! A SUFFERER TALKS ABOUT RESTLESS LEGS SYNDROME, by Sara Burns, Reprinted with permission from Volume 2, Number 4, July/August 2002, issue of the Journal of the American Association for Medical Transcription.

YOU'RE DOING WHAT? THE PITFALLS AND REWARDS OF LIVING YOUR DREAM, by Sara Burns,. Reprinted with permission from Volume 22, Number 5, September/October 2003, issue of the Journal of the American Association for Medical Transcription.

TIDBITS FROM 25 YEARS AS A HOME-BASED MEDICAL TRANSCRIPTIONIST — WHAT I HOPE I HAVE LEARNED, by Sara Burns. Reprinted with permission from Volume 23, Number 2, March/April, 2004, (Part I) and Volume 23, Number 3, May/June 2004 (Part II) issues of the Journal of the American Association for Medical Transcription.

IN DEFENSE OF DOCTORS — SOME PROS AND CONS ON THE BALANCE SHEET, by Sara Burns. Reprinted with permission from Plexus, Volume 1, Issue 6, September 2005.

IN SEARCH OF THE PERFECT SUBCONTRACTOR — JUST ANOTHER WAY TO COMPLICATE AND AGGRAVATE YOUR LIFE, by Sara Burns. Reprinted with permission from Plexus, Volume 2, Issue 5, September 2006.

ROBERT D. REED PUBLISHERS ORDER FORM

Call in your order for fast service and quantity discounts!
(541) 347- 9882
OR order on-line at www.rdrpublishers.com using PayPal.
OR order by mail: Make a copy of this form; enclose payment information:
Robert D. Reed Publishers
1380 Face Rock Drive, Bandon, OR 97411
Note: Shipping is $3.50 1st book + $1 for each additional book.

Send indicated books to:
Name: _____
Address: _____
City: _____ State: _____ Zip: _____
Phone: _____ Fax: _____ Cell: _____
E-Mail: _____
Payment by check ☐ or credit card ☐ (*All major credit cards are accepted*)
Name on card: _____
Card Number: _____
Exp. Date: _____ Last 3-Digit number on back of card: _____
Quantity: _____ Total Amount: _____

You're a Medical What? A Lighthearted Peek into the
World of a Medical Transcriptionist
by Sara Burns ....$14.95 _____

Handling Employment BS
by Geoffrey Hopper .... $19.95 _____

100 Ways to Create Wealth
by Steve Chandler & Sam Beckford .... $24.95 _____

The Secret of Transitions: How to Move Effortlessly to
Higher Levels of Success
by Jim Manton .... $14.95_____

Customer Astonishment
by Darby Checketts ....$14.95_____

Ten Commitments for Building High Performance Teams
by Tom Massey .... $11.95 _____

Other book title(s) from website:
_____ $ _____
_____   _____